# 50 Small Bites and Finger Foods Recipes for Home

By: Kelly Johnson

# Table of Contents

- BBQ Pulled Pork Sliders
- Ceviche Shooters
- Mini BLT Sandwiches
- Stuffed Mini Bell Peppers with Cream Cheese and Bacon
- Avocado Shrimp Cups
- Chicken Caesar Salad Cups
- Mini Crab Cakes with Lemon Aioli
- Greek Meatball Skewers with Tzatziki Sauce
- Mini Sausage Rolls
- Mushroom Bruschetta
- Teriyaki Tofu Skewers
- Cranberry Turkey Pinwheels
- Mini Chicken Pot Pies
- Smoked Gouda and Bacon Stuffed Mushrooms
- Chocolate-Dipped Strawberries

**Mini Caprese Skewers**

Ingredients:

- Cherry or grape tomatoes
- Fresh mozzarella balls (bocconcini)
- Fresh basil leaves
- Balsamic glaze (store-bought or homemade)
- Toothpicks or small skewers

Instructions:

Rinse the cherry or grape tomatoes and pat them dry with paper towels.

Drain the fresh mozzarella balls if they were stored in water, then pat them dry as well.

Take a toothpick or small skewer and thread on a tomato, followed by a basil leaf (folded or rolled up if large), and finally a mozzarella ball.

Repeat the process until you have assembled all the skewers.

Arrange the mini Caprese skewers on a serving platter.

Drizzle balsamic glaze over the skewers just before serving. If you're making your own glaze, you can reduce balsamic vinegar in a saucepan over low heat until it thickens to a syrupy consistency.

Serve immediately and enjoy!

These Mini Caprese Skewers are not only visually appealing but also bursting with fresh flavors. They're perfect for parties, gatherings, or even as a light snack any time of the day. Enjoy!

**Spinach and Feta Stuffed Mushrooms**

Ingredients:

- 12 large mushrooms, stems removed and reserved
- 2 cups fresh spinach, chopped
- 1/2 cup crumbled feta cheese
- 2 cloves garlic, minced
- 2 tablespoons olive oil
- Salt and pepper to taste
- Grated Parmesan cheese for topping (optional)
- Chopped fresh parsley for garnish (optional)

Instructions:

Preheat your oven to 375°F (190°C). Line a baking sheet with parchment paper or lightly grease it.

Clean the mushrooms with a damp paper towel to remove any dirt. Carefully remove the stems from the mushrooms and finely chop them.

Heat olive oil in a skillet over medium heat. Add the chopped mushroom stems and minced garlic. Cook for 2-3 minutes until the mushrooms are softened and the garlic is fragrant.

Add the chopped spinach to the skillet and cook until wilted, about 2-3 minutes. Season with salt and pepper to taste.

Remove the skillet from heat and let the mixture cool slightly. Once cooled, stir in the crumbled feta cheese.

Stuff each mushroom cap with the spinach and feta mixture, pressing down gently to pack it in.

Place the stuffed mushrooms on the prepared baking sheet. If desired, sprinkle grated Parmesan cheese over the tops of the mushrooms.

Bake in the preheated oven for 15-20 minutes, or until the mushrooms are tender and the filling is heated through.

Remove from the oven and let cool for a few minutes before serving.

Garnish with chopped fresh parsley, if desired, and serve warm.

These Spinach and Feta Stuffed Mushrooms are packed with flavor and make a fantastic appetizer or party snack. Enjoy!

**Bacon-Wrapped Dates**

Ingredients:

- 12 Medjool dates, pitted
- 6 slices of bacon, cut in half crosswise
- 24 whole almonds (optional)
- Toothpicks or cocktail sticks

Instructions:

Preheat your oven to 375°F (190°C). Line a baking sheet with parchment paper or aluminum foil.

If using almonds, stuff each date with a whole almond. This step is optional but adds a nice crunch to the center of the dates.

Wrap each stuffed date with a half slice of bacon, ensuring it covers the date completely. Secure the bacon in place by inserting a toothpick through the center.

Place the bacon-wrapped dates on the prepared baking sheet, seam side down.

Bake in the preheated oven for 15-20 minutes, or until the bacon is crispy and golden brown.

Once cooked, remove the toothpicks from the bacon-wrapped dates.

Allow the dates to cool for a few minutes before serving.

Serve warm as an appetizer or snack.

These Bacon-Wrapped Dates are a perfect combination of sweet, salty, and savory

flavors, making them a hit at any party or gathering. Enjoy!

**Chicken Satay Skewers with Peanut Sauce**

Ingredients:

For Chicken Satay:

- 1 pound boneless, skinless chicken breasts or thighs, cut into thin strips
- 1 tablespoon soy sauce
- 1 tablespoon fish sauce
- 1 tablespoon brown sugar
- 1 tablespoon curry powder
- 1 teaspoon turmeric powder
- 2 cloves garlic, minced
- 1 tablespoon vegetable oil
- Wooden skewers, soaked in water for 30 minutes

For Peanut Sauce:

- 1/2 cup creamy peanut butter
- 1/4 cup coconut milk
- 2 tablespoons soy sauce
- 1 tablespoon brown sugar
- 1 tablespoon lime juice
- 1 clove garlic, minced
- 1 teaspoon sriracha or chili sauce (adjust to taste)
- Water (as needed to adjust consistency)

For Garnish (optional):

- Chopped peanuts
- Chopped cilantro
- Lime wedges

Instructions:

Marinate the Chicken: In a bowl, combine soy sauce, fish sauce, brown sugar, curry powder, turmeric powder, minced garlic, and vegetable oil. Add the chicken strips and toss to coat. Let it marinate for at least 30 minutes or up to overnight in the refrigerator.

Make Peanut Sauce: In a saucepan over medium heat, combine peanut butter, coconut milk, soy sauce, brown sugar, lime juice, minced garlic, and sriracha. Stir continuously until well combined and heated through. If the sauce is too thick, you can thin it out with a little water until you reach your desired consistency. Set aside.

Preheat Grill or Grill Pan: Preheat your grill or grill pan over medium-high heat. If you're using wooden skewers, make sure to soak them in water for at least 30 minutes to prevent them from burning.

Assemble the Skewers: Thread the marinated chicken strips onto the skewers, leaving a little space between each piece.

Grill the Skewers: Place the chicken skewers on the preheated grill or grill pan. Cook for about 3-4 minutes on each side, or until the chicken is cooked through and has nice grill marks.

Serve: Transfer the cooked skewers to a serving platter. Serve hot with the prepared peanut sauce on the side. You can sprinkle chopped peanuts and cilantro on top for garnish if desired. Serve with lime wedges for an extra burst of flavor.

Enjoy your delicious chicken satay skewers with peanut sauce! They make a fantastic appetizer or main dish for any occasion.

**Mini Quiches**

Ingredients:

- 1 package of pre-made pie crust dough (or you can make your own)
- 4 large eggs
- 1/2 cup milk or heavy cream
- 1/2 cup shredded cheese (such as cheddar, Swiss, or Gruyere)
- 1/2 cup diced vegetables (such as spinach, bell peppers, onions, mushrooms, etc.)
- Salt and pepper to taste
- Optional: cooked bacon, ham, or sausage, diced
- Optional: fresh herbs like parsley, chives, or thyme, chopped

Instructions:

Preheat Oven: Preheat your oven to 375°F (190°C). Lightly grease a mini muffin tin or line it with mini muffin liners.

Prepare Pie Crust: Roll out the pie crust dough on a lightly floured surface. Using a cookie cutter or a glass, cut out circles slightly larger than the muffin tin cavities. Press each circle of dough into the cavities, making sure to form a small cup shape.

Prepare Filling: In a mixing bowl, whisk together the eggs and milk or cream until well combined. Season with salt and pepper to taste. Stir in the shredded cheese, diced vegetables, and any optional add-ins like cooked bacon, ham, or sausage.

Fill the Crusts: Spoon the egg mixture into each prepared crust, filling them nearly to the top. Be careful not to overfill.

Bake: Place the muffin tin in the preheated oven and bake for about 15-20 minutes, or until the quiches are set and the crust is golden brown.

Cool and Serve: Remove the mini quiches from the oven and allow them to cool in the muffin tin for a few minutes. Then, carefully transfer them to a wire rack to cool completely. Serve warm or at room temperature.

Garnish (Optional): If desired, garnish the mini quiches with chopped fresh herbs before serving.

Enjoy these delicious mini quiches as a tasty appetizer or snack! They can be customized with your favorite fillings to suit your taste preferences.

**Cheese Stuffed Jalapeno Poppers**

Ingredients:

- 12 fresh jalapeño peppers
- 8 ounces cream cheese, softened
- 1 cup shredded cheddar cheese (or your preferred cheese blend)
- 1/2 teaspoon garlic powder
- 1/2 teaspoon onion powder
- 1/2 teaspoon paprika
- Salt and black pepper, to taste
- 6 slices of bacon, cut in half (optional)
- Toothpicks

Instructions:

Preheat Oven: Preheat your oven to 375°F (190°C). Line a baking sheet with parchment paper or aluminum foil for easy cleanup.

Prepare Jalapeños: Wash the jalapeño peppers and cut them in half lengthwise. Use a spoon to carefully remove the seeds and membranes from each half, creating small pepper boats.

Prepare Filling: In a mixing bowl, combine the softened cream cheese, shredded cheddar cheese, garlic powder, onion powder, paprika, salt, and black pepper. Mix until well combined.

Stuff Jalapeños: Spoon the cheese mixture into each jalapeño half, filling them evenly. Press the filling down gently to ensure it stays in place.

Wrap with Bacon (Optional): If using bacon, wrap each stuffed jalapeño half with a half-slice of bacon and secure it with a toothpick. This step is optional but adds an extra layer of flavor.

Bake: Place the stuffed jalapeños on the prepared baking sheet. Bake in the preheated oven for about 20-25 minutes, or until the peppers are tender, the cheese is melted and bubbly, and the bacon is crispy.

Serve: Once cooked, remove the jalapeño poppers from the oven and let them cool slightly before serving. Be cautious when handling them, as they may be hot. Serve warm and enjoy!

These cheese-stuffed jalapeño poppers are sure to be a hit at your next gathering.

They're spicy, creamy, and packed with flavor. You can adjust the level of heat by

removing more or less of the jalapeño seeds and membranes. Enjoy!

**Bruschetta with Tomato and Basil**

Ingredients:

- 4-6 ripe tomatoes, diced
- 1/4 cup fresh basil leaves, chopped
- 2 cloves garlic, minced
- 2 tablespoons extra virgin olive oil
- 1 tablespoon balsamic vinegar (optional)
- Salt and pepper, to taste
- 1 French baguette, sliced into 1/2-inch thick slices
- Olive oil, for brushing
- Optional: Balsamic glaze for drizzling

Instructions:

Prepare Tomato Basil Mixture: In a bowl, combine the diced tomatoes, chopped basil, minced garlic, extra virgin olive oil, and balsamic vinegar (if using). Season with salt and pepper to taste. Mix well and set aside to let the flavors meld together.

Toast Baguette Slices: Preheat your oven broiler or grill pan. Brush the sliced baguette with olive oil on both sides. Place the slices on a baking sheet or directly on the grill pan and toast them until they are lightly golden brown and crispy on the edges. Watch them closely to prevent burning, as they can toast quickly.

Top with Tomato Basil Mixture: Once the baguette slices are toasted, remove them from the oven or grill pan. Spoon a generous amount of the tomato basil mixture onto each slice, spreading it evenly.

Serve: Arrange the bruschetta slices on a serving platter and serve immediately. If desired, drizzle a little balsamic glaze over the top for added flavor and presentation.

Optional Garnish: You can garnish the bruschetta with additional fresh basil leaves or a sprinkle of grated Parmesan cheese before serving.

Enjoy this delicious and fresh bruschetta with tomato and basil as a starter, appetizer, or light snack. It's perfect for any occasion and sure to impress your guests with its vibrant colors and flavors. Buon appetito!

**Mini Meatballs with Marinara Sauce**

Ingredients:

For Meatballs:

- 1 pound ground beef (or a mixture of beef and pork)
- 1/2 cup breadcrumbs
- 1/4 cup grated Parmesan cheese
- 1 egg
- 2 cloves garlic, minced
- 1 teaspoon dried oregano
- 1 teaspoon dried basil
- 1/2 teaspoon salt
- 1/4 teaspoon black pepper
- Olive oil (for frying)

For Marinara Sauce:

- 1 tablespoon olive oil
- 1 small onion, finely chopped
- 2 cloves garlic, minced
- 1 can (14 ounces) crushed tomatoes
- 1 teaspoon dried oregano
- 1 teaspoon dried basil
- Salt and pepper, to taste
- Pinch of sugar (optional, to balance acidity)

Instructions:

Prepare Meatballs: In a large mixing bowl, combine the ground beef, breadcrumbs, grated Parmesan cheese, egg, minced garlic, dried oregano, dried basil, salt, and black pepper. Mix until all ingredients are well combined.
Form Meatballs: Take small portions of the meat mixture and roll them into mini meatballs, about 1 inch in diameter. You should get approximately 20-24 mini meatballs from this recipe.
Cook Meatballs: Heat a drizzle of olive oil in a large skillet over medium heat. Once the oil is hot, add the meatballs in a single layer, making sure not to overcrowd the pan. You may need to work in batches. Cook the meatballs for about 8-10 minutes, turning occasionally, until they are browned on all sides and

cooked through. Transfer the cooked meatballs to a plate lined with paper towels to drain excess oil.

Prepare Marinara Sauce: In the same skillet, add another tablespoon of olive oil if needed. Add the finely chopped onion and minced garlic, and sauté until softened and translucent, about 2-3 minutes. Pour in the crushed tomatoes and add the dried oregano and dried basil. Season with salt, pepper, and a pinch of sugar (if using) to taste. Stir well to combine.

Simmer Sauce: Reduce the heat to low and let the marinara sauce simmer for about 10-15 minutes, stirring occasionally, to allow the flavors to meld together and the sauce to thicken slightly.

Serve: Once the marinara sauce is ready, add the cooked meatballs back to the skillet and toss gently to coat them with the sauce. Let them simmer together for a few minutes to heat through.

Serve Hot: Transfer the mini meatballs with marinara sauce to a serving dish and serve hot. Optionally, garnish with chopped fresh parsley or grated Parmesan cheese before serving.

Enjoy these delicious mini meatballs with marinara sauce as an appetizer with toothpicks or serve them over pasta for a satisfying main dish. They're sure to be a crowd-pleaser!

**Crab Cakes with Remoulade Sauce**

Ingredients:

For Crab Cakes:

- 1 pound lump crab meat, picked over for shells
- 1/2 cup breadcrumbs
- 1/4 cup mayonnaise
- 1 large egg, beaten
- 2 tablespoons Dijon mustard
- 2 tablespoons chopped fresh parsley
- 1 tablespoon Worcestershire sauce
- 1 teaspoon Old Bay seasoning (or more to taste)
- 1/4 teaspoon salt
- 1/4 teaspoon black pepper
- 1/4 cup vegetable oil (for frying)

For Remoulade Sauce:

- 1/2 cup mayonnaise
- 2 tablespoons Dijon mustard
- 1 tablespoon capers, drained and chopped
- 1 tablespoon chopped fresh parsley
- 1 tablespoon chopped green onions (scallions)
- 1 tablespoon chopped dill pickle or cornichons
- 1 tablespoon lemon juice
- 1 teaspoon Worcestershire sauce
- 1 teaspoon paprika
- Salt and black pepper, to taste

Instructions:

Prepare Crab Cakes Mixture: In a large mixing bowl, combine the lump crab meat, breadcrumbs, mayonnaise, beaten egg, Dijon mustard, chopped parsley, Worcestershire sauce, Old Bay seasoning, salt, and black pepper. Gently fold the ingredients together until well combined, being careful not to break up the crab meat too much.

Form Crab Cakes: Divide the crab mixture into equal portions and shape them into round patties, about 1/2 inch thick. You should get approximately 8 crab cakes from this recipe. Place them on a plate lined with parchment paper and refrigerate for at least 30 minutes to firm up.

Prepare Remoulade Sauce: In a small bowl, whisk together the mayonnaise, Dijon mustard, chopped capers, chopped parsley, chopped green onions, chopped dill pickle, lemon juice, Worcestershire sauce, paprika, salt, and black pepper. Taste and adjust seasoning as needed. Cover the sauce and refrigerate until ready to serve.

Cook Crab Cakes: Heat vegetable oil in a large skillet over medium-high heat. Once the oil is hot, carefully place the crab cakes in the skillet, working in batches if necessary to avoid overcrowding. Cook the crab cakes for about 3-4 minutes on each side, or until they are golden brown and crispy on the outside and heated through.

Serve: Transfer the cooked crab cakes to a serving platter. Serve hot, accompanied by the prepared remoulade sauce on the side for dipping or drizzling.

Garnish (Optional): Garnish the crab cakes with additional chopped parsley or a squeeze of lemon juice before serving for added freshness.

Enjoy these delicious crab cakes with remoulade sauce as a delightful appetizer or main course. They're perfect for any occasion and are sure to impress your guests with their irresistible flavor!

**Vegetable Spring Rolls with Sweet Chili Dipping Sauce**

Ingredients:

For Vegetable Spring Rolls:

- 8-10 spring roll wrappers (also called rice paper wrappers)
- 2 cups shredded cabbage
- 1 cup shredded carrots
- 1 cup bean sprouts
- 1 bell pepper, thinly sliced
- 1 cucumber, julienned
- 1 avocado, sliced (optional)
- Fresh mint leaves
- Fresh cilantro leaves
- Cooked vermicelli noodles (optional)

For Sweet Chili Dipping Sauce:

- 1/4 cup sweet chili sauce
- 2 tablespoons soy sauce
- 1 tablespoon rice vinegar
- 1 teaspoon sesame oil
- 1 clove garlic, minced
- 1 teaspoon grated ginger
- Red pepper flakes, to taste (optional)

Instructions:

Prepare Ingredients: Prepare all the vegetables by shredding, slicing, and julienning them as mentioned in the ingredient list. Cook vermicelli noodles according to package instructions if using.

Prepare Dipping Sauce: In a small bowl, whisk together the sweet chili sauce, soy sauce, rice vinegar, sesame oil, minced garlic, grated ginger, and red pepper flakes (if using). Adjust seasoning to taste. Set aside.

Prepare Spring Roll Wrappers: Fill a shallow dish or pie plate with warm water. Working with one spring roll wrapper at a time, dip it into the water for about 10-15 seconds until it softens. Be careful not to oversoak, as the wrapper will become too delicate.

Assemble Spring Rolls: Place the softened wrapper on a clean, damp kitchen towel or a plate. Arrange a small portion of each vegetable filling in the center of the wrapper, leaving some space at the edges. Optionally, add a slice of avocado and a few pieces of cooked vermicelli noodles. Top with a few mint and cilantro leaves.

Roll Spring Rolls: Fold the sides of the wrapper over the filling, then fold the bottom edge up and over the filling, tucking it tightly. Roll the spring roll upwards, pressing gently to seal the edge. Repeat with the remaining wrappers and filling.

Serve: Arrange the vegetable spring rolls on a serving platter. Serve with the prepared sweet chili dipping sauce on the side.

Garnish (Optional): Garnish the spring rolls with additional fresh herbs or sesame seeds for extra flavor and presentation.

Enjoy these delicious vegetable spring rolls with sweet chili dipping sauce as a light and refreshing appetizer or snack! They're perfect for parties, gatherings, or even a healthy lunch option.

**Mini Grilled Cheese Sandwiches**

Ingredients:

- Sliced bread (white or whole wheat)
- Cheddar cheese, sliced
- Butter, softened

Instructions:

Prepare Bread: Lay out the slices of bread on a clean work surface. You can trim the crusts off if you prefer, but it's optional.

Assemble Sandwiches: Place a slice of cheddar cheese between two slices of bread to form sandwiches.

Butter Bread: Spread a thin layer of softened butter on one side of each sandwich. This will help the bread toast evenly and develop a golden crust when grilled.

Heat Skillet or Pan: Heat a skillet or frying pan over medium heat. You can also use a griddle if you have one.

Grill Sandwiches: Once the skillet is hot, carefully place the buttered side of the sandwiches down onto the skillet. Cook for about 2-3 minutes, or until the bottom side is golden brown and the cheese begins to melt.

Flip and Cook: Using a spatula, carefully flip the sandwiches over and cook the other side for another 2-3 minutes, or until golden brown and the cheese is fully melted.

Serve: Once both sides are golden brown and the cheese is melted, remove the mini grilled cheese sandwiches from the skillet and transfer them to a cutting board. Let them cool for a minute or two before cutting them into smaller pieces, if desired.

Serve Hot: Arrange the mini grilled cheese sandwiches on a serving platter and serve hot. Optionally, you can pair them with tomato soup for dipping or serve with a side of your favorite condiment.

Enjoy these delicious mini grilled cheese sandwiches as a tasty appetizer or snack that's sure to please both kids and adults alike! Feel free to customize them by adding other ingredients like ham, bacon, tomato slices, or different types of cheese.

**Shrimp Cocktail Shooters**

Ingredients:

- 1 pound large shrimp, peeled and deveined
- Cocktail sauce (store-bought or homemade)
- Lemon wedges, for garnish
- Fresh parsley or cilantro, for garnish
- Toothpicks or small skewers

For Cocktail Sauce:

- 1/2 cup ketchup
- 2 tablespoons prepared horseradish (adjust to taste)
- 1 tablespoon lemon juice
- 1 teaspoon Worcestershire sauce
- Hot sauce, to taste (optional)
- Salt and pepper, to taste

Instructions:

Prepare Shrimp: Fill a large pot with water and bring it to a boil. Add the peeled and deveined shrimp to the boiling water and cook for 2-3 minutes, or until they turn pink and opaque. Be careful not to overcook them, as shrimp can become tough if cooked for too long. Once cooked, immediately transfer the shrimp to a bowl of ice water to stop the cooking process. Drain the shrimp and pat them dry with paper towels.

Prepare Cocktail Sauce: In a small bowl, mix together the ketchup, prepared horseradish, lemon juice, Worcestershire sauce, hot sauce (if using), salt, and pepper. Adjust the amount of horseradish and hot sauce to suit your taste preferences. Cover and refrigerate the cocktail sauce until ready to use.

Assemble Shrimp Cocktail Shooters: Arrange small shot glasses or serving vessels on a serving platter. Place a dollop of cocktail sauce into the bottom of each glass.

Skewer Shrimp: Skewer each cooked shrimp with a toothpick or small skewer. Place one shrimp skewer into each shot glass on top of the cocktail sauce.

Garnish: Garnish the shrimp cocktail shooters with a squeeze of lemon juice and a sprig of fresh parsley or cilantro.

Serve: Arrange the shrimp cocktail shooters on a serving platter and serve immediately. Optionally, you can serve them with additional lemon wedges and cocktail sauce on the side for dipping.

Enjoy these elegant shrimp cocktail shooters as a delicious appetizer that's both visually stunning and flavorful. They're sure to impress your guests at any gathering!

**Buffalo Chicken Bites with Blue Cheese Dip**

Ingredients:

For Buffalo Chicken Bites:

- 1 pound boneless, skinless chicken breasts, cut into bite-sized pieces
- 1/2 cup all-purpose flour
- 1/2 teaspoon garlic powder
- 1/2 teaspoon onion powder
- Salt and pepper, to taste
- 1/4 cup hot sauce (such as Frank's RedHot)
- 2 tablespoons unsalted butter, melted
- Cooking spray

For Blue Cheese Dip:

- 1/2 cup mayonnaise
- 1/2 cup sour cream
- 1/2 cup crumbled blue cheese
- 1 tablespoon lemon juice
- 1/2 teaspoon garlic powder
- Salt and pepper, to taste
- Chopped fresh parsley or chives, for garnish (optional)

Instructions:

Preheat Oven: Preheat your oven to 400°F (200°C). Line a baking sheet with parchment paper and lightly coat it with cooking spray.

Prepare Chicken: In a shallow dish, combine the all-purpose flour, garlic powder, onion powder, salt, and pepper. Dredge the chicken pieces in the flour mixture, shaking off any excess.

Bake Chicken: Place the coated chicken pieces on the prepared baking sheet in a single layer. Bake in the preheated oven for 15-20 minutes, or until the chicken is cooked through and golden brown.

Prepare Buffalo Sauce: In a small bowl, mix together the hot sauce and melted butter until well combined.

Coat Chicken in Buffalo Sauce: Once the chicken is cooked, transfer it to a large mixing bowl. Pour the buffalo sauce over the chicken and toss until all the pieces are evenly coated.

Make Blue Cheese Dip: In another bowl, mix together the mayonnaise, sour cream, crumbled blue cheese, lemon juice, garlic powder, salt, and pepper until smooth and creamy. Adjust seasoning to taste.

Serve: Arrange the buffalo chicken bites on a serving platter. Garnish with chopped fresh parsley or chives if desired. Serve hot with the blue cheese dip on the side for dipping.

Enjoy: Enjoy these delicious buffalo chicken bites with blue cheese dip as a crowd-pleasing appetizer or snack!

These buffalo chicken bites are sure to be a hit at any party or gathering. The tangy buffalo sauce pairs perfectly with the creamy blue cheese dip for a flavor combination that's simply irresistible.

**Deviled Eggs**

Ingredients:

- 6 large eggs
- 3 tablespoons mayonnaise
- 1 teaspoon Dijon mustard
- 1/2 teaspoon white vinegar or lemon juice
- Salt and pepper, to taste
- Paprika, for garnish
- Optional toppings: chopped chives, crispy bacon bits, diced pickles, smoked paprika, or sliced olives

Instructions:

Hard Boil Eggs: Place the eggs in a single layer in a saucepan and cover with water. Bring the water to a boil over medium-high heat. Once boiling, cover the saucepan and remove it from the heat. Let the eggs sit in the hot water for 12 minutes.

Cool Eggs: After 12 minutes, carefully transfer the eggs to a bowl of ice water to cool completely. This will stop the cooking process and make the eggs easier to peel. Let them sit in the ice water bath for about 10 minutes.

Peel Eggs: Gently tap each egg on a hard surface to crack the shell, then peel off the shell under cool running water. Pat the peeled eggs dry with a paper towel.

Slice Eggs: Once peeled, slice each egg in half lengthwise. Carefully remove the yolks and transfer them to a mixing bowl. Arrange the egg white halves on a serving platter.

Prepare Filling: Mash the egg yolks with a fork until smooth. Add the mayonnaise, Dijon mustard, white vinegar or lemon juice, salt, and pepper to the mashed yolks. Stir until well combined and creamy. Adjust seasoning to taste.

Fill Egg Whites: Spoon or pipe the yolk mixture into the hollows of the egg white halves. You can use a spoon or a piping bag fitted with a star tip for a decorative touch.

Garnish: Sprinkle the filled deviled eggs with paprika for a classic finish. You can also garnish with any optional toppings like chopped chives, crispy bacon bits, diced pickles, smoked paprika, or sliced olives.

Chill and Serve: Once assembled, refrigerate the deviled eggs for at least 30 minutes to allow the flavors to meld together. Serve chilled as a delicious appetizer or side dish.

Enjoy these classic deviled eggs as a tasty addition to any meal or gathering. They're easy to customize with your favorite toppings and are always a hit with guests!

**Teriyaki Chicken Wings**

Ingredients:

For Teriyaki Sauce:

- 1/2 cup soy sauce
- 1/4 cup water
- 1/4 cup brown sugar
- 2 tablespoons honey
- 2 cloves garlic, minced
- 1 teaspoon grated ginger
- 1 tablespoon cornstarch (optional, for thickening)
- 1 tablespoon water (optional, for cornstarch slurry)

For Chicken Wings:

- 2 pounds chicken wings, separated into drumettes and flats
- Salt and pepper, to taste
- Vegetable oil, for frying
- Sesame seeds, for garnish (optional)
- Sliced green onions, for garnish (optional)

Instructions:

Prepare Teriyaki Sauce: In a small saucepan, combine soy sauce, water, brown sugar, honey, minced garlic, and grated ginger. Bring the mixture to a simmer over medium heat, stirring occasionally until the sugar has dissolved. If you prefer a thicker sauce, you can mix cornstarch with water to make a slurry and add it to the sauce, stirring constantly until thickened. Remove from heat and set aside.

Prepare Chicken Wings: Pat the chicken wings dry with paper towels to remove excess moisture. Season the wings with salt and pepper to taste.

Fry Chicken Wings: In a large skillet or deep fryer, heat vegetable oil to 375°F (190°C). Carefully add the chicken wings to the hot oil in batches, making sure not to overcrowd the pan. Fry the wings for about 8-10 minutes, turning occasionally, or until they are golden brown and crispy.

Coat Wings in Teriyaki Sauce: Once the chicken wings are cooked through and crispy, transfer them to a large bowl. Pour the prepared teriyaki sauce over the wings and toss to coat them evenly.

Garnish and Serve: Arrange the teriyaki chicken wings on a serving platter. Sprinkle with sesame seeds and sliced green onions for garnish, if desired.

Serve Hot: Serve the teriyaki chicken wings hot as a delicious appetizer or main dish. They're perfect for parties, game day, or as a flavorful addition to any meal.

Enjoy these tasty teriyaki chicken wings with their sweet and savory glaze, sure to satisfy your cravings for delicious Asian-inspired flavors!

**Spanakopita Triangles**

Ingredients:

- 1 package (16 ounces) frozen phyllo pastry sheets, thawed
- 10 ounces fresh spinach, chopped (or 1 package frozen spinach, thawed and drained)
- 1 cup crumbled feta cheese
- 1/2 cup finely chopped onions
- 2 cloves garlic, minced
- 1/4 cup chopped fresh dill (or 1 tablespoon dried dill)
- 1/4 cup chopped fresh parsley
- 1/4 cup olive oil, plus more for brushing
- Salt and pepper, to taste

Instructions:

Prepare Filling: If using fresh spinach, blanch it in boiling water for 1-2 minutes, then drain and squeeze out excess moisture. If using frozen spinach, make sure it is thawed and well-drained. In a large mixing bowl, combine the spinach, crumbled feta cheese, chopped onions, minced garlic, chopped dill, chopped parsley, and olive oil. Season with salt and pepper to taste. Mix well to combine.
Preheat Oven: Preheat your oven to 375°F (190°C). Line a baking sheet with parchment paper.
Assemble Spanakopita Triangles: Carefully unroll the phyllo pastry sheets on a clean work surface. Keep them covered with a slightly damp kitchen towel to prevent them from drying out. Working with one sheet at a time, brush it lightly with olive oil. Place another sheet on top and brush with olive oil again. Repeat until you have 4 layers of phyllo pastry.
Cut Phyllo Sheets: Use a sharp knife to cut the layered phyllo sheets into strips, about 3 inches wide. Place a spoonful of the spinach and feta filling at one end of each strip.
Fold into Triangles: Fold one corner of the phyllo strip over the filling to form a triangle. Continue folding the triangle over itself, as you would fold a flag, until you reach the end of the strip. Press the edges to seal. Repeat with the remaining phyllo strips and filling.
Bake: Place the spanakopita triangles on the prepared baking sheet. Brush the tops with olive oil. Bake in the preheated oven for 20-25 minutes, or until the pastry is golden brown and crispy.

Serve: Once baked, remove the spanakopita triangles from the oven and let them cool slightly before serving. They can be served warm or at room temperature.

Enjoy these delicious spanakopita triangles as a flavorful appetizer or snack. They're perfect for parties, gatherings, or as a tasty addition to a Greek-themed meal!

**Smoked Salmon and Cream Cheese Cucumber Bites**

Ingredients:

- 1 English cucumber
- 4 ounces smoked salmon, thinly sliced
- 4 ounces cream cheese, softened
- 1 tablespoon fresh dill, chopped
- 1 tablespoon capers, drained
- 1 teaspoon lemon juice
- Salt and pepper, to taste
- Optional garnish: fresh dill sprigs, lemon zest

Instructions:

Prepare Cucumber: Wash the cucumber thoroughly and slice it into rounds, about 1/4 inch thick. You can leave the skin on for added color and texture, or peel it if you prefer.

Prepare Cream Cheese Mixture: In a small bowl, mix together the softened cream cheese, chopped fresh dill, drained capers, and lemon juice. Season with salt and pepper to taste. Stir until well combined.

Assemble Cucumber Bites: Place the cucumber slices on a serving platter. Spread a thin layer of the cream cheese mixture on each cucumber slice.

Add Smoked Salmon: Tear or cut the smoked salmon slices into smaller pieces. Place a piece of smoked salmon on top of each cucumber slice with cream cheese.

Garnish (Optional): Garnish the smoked salmon and cream cheese cucumber bites with additional fresh dill sprigs and lemon zest for extra flavor and presentation.

Serve: Arrange the cucumber bites on a serving platter and serve immediately. Optionally, you can chill them in the refrigerator for 15-30 minutes before serving to allow the flavors to meld together.

Enjoy these delightful smoked salmon and cream cheese cucumber bites as a delicious and elegant appetizer that's sure to impress your guests with its vibrant colors and fresh flavors!

**Chicken and Waffle Sliders**

Ingredients:

For the Chicken:

- 1 pound boneless, skinless chicken breasts
- 1 cup buttermilk
- 1 cup all-purpose flour
- 1 teaspoon salt
- 1 teaspoon pepper
- 1 teaspoon paprika
- 1/2 teaspoon garlic powder
- Vegetable oil, for frying

For the Waffles:

- 2 cups all-purpose flour
- 2 tablespoons granulated sugar
- 1 tablespoon baking powder
- 1/2 teaspoon salt
- 1 3/4 cups milk
- 1/3 cup vegetable oil
- 2 large eggs
- 1 teaspoon vanilla extract

For Assembly:

- Maple syrup
- Optional toppings: sliced cheese, crispy bacon, lettuce, tomato, avocado, etc.

Instructions:

Chicken:

Cut the chicken breasts into small, slider-sized pieces.
In a bowl, mix together buttermilk, salt, pepper, paprika, and garlic powder.
Place the chicken pieces in the buttermilk mixture, ensuring they are fully coated.
Marinate for at least 30 minutes, or overnight for best results.
In a separate shallow dish, mix together flour, salt, pepper, paprika, and garlic powder.
Heat vegetable oil in a large skillet over medium-high heat.

Remove chicken from buttermilk mixture, allowing excess to drip off, then dredge in the flour mixture, coating evenly.
Fry the chicken in batches until golden brown and cooked through, about 3-4 minutes per side. Transfer to a paper towel-lined plate to drain excess oil.

Waffles:

Preheat your waffle iron according to manufacturer's instructions.
In a large bowl, whisk together flour, sugar, baking powder, and salt.
In another bowl, whisk together milk, vegetable oil, eggs, and vanilla extract.
Pour the wet ingredients into the dry ingredients and stir until just combined. Be careful not to overmix; it's okay if there are a few lumps.
Cook waffles according to your waffle iron's instructions until golden brown and crisp.

Assembly:

Once the chicken and waffles are ready, cut the waffles into slider-sized squares.
Place a piece of fried chicken on one waffle square, then drizzle with maple syrup.
Top with another waffle square to create a sandwich.
Optionally, add any desired toppings such as cheese, bacon, lettuce, tomato, or avocado.
Secure each slider with a toothpick and serve warm.

Enjoy your delicious chicken and waffle sliders! They're sure to be a hit at any gathering.

**Stuffed Cherry Tomatoes with Herbed Cream Cheese**

Ingredients:

- 24 cherry tomatoes
- 8 ounces cream cheese, softened
- 2 tablespoons finely chopped fresh herbs (such as chives, parsley, dill, or basil)
- 1 tablespoon finely chopped green onions (optional)
- Salt and pepper to taste
- Optional garnish: additional chopped herbs or paprika

Instructions:

Prepare the Cherry Tomatoes:
- Wash the cherry tomatoes and pat them dry with a paper towel.
- Slice off the top of each tomato and discard. Use a small spoon or a melon baller to scoop out the seeds and pulp from each tomato, leaving the shell intact. You want to create a small cavity in each tomato for the filling.

Make the Herbed Cream Cheese:
- In a mixing bowl, combine the softened cream cheese, finely chopped herbs, and green onions (if using).
- Season the mixture with salt and pepper to taste. Mix until the herbs are evenly distributed throughout the cream cheese.

Stuff the Tomatoes:
- Use a small spoon or a piping bag to fill each hollowed-out cherry tomato with the herbed cream cheese mixture. Fill them until the cream cheese is slightly mounded on top.

Garnish and Serve:
- If desired, garnish the stuffed cherry tomatoes with additional chopped herbs or a sprinkle of paprika for color.
- Arrange the stuffed cherry tomatoes on a serving platter and refrigerate for at least 30 minutes to allow the flavors to meld and the cream cheese to set.
- Serve chilled as a delicious appetizer or snack. Enjoy!

These stuffed cherry tomatoes are not only tasty but also visually appealing, making them a perfect addition to any party spread or gathering. Feel free to customize the herbed cream cheese filling with your favorite herbs and seasonings for a unique flavor profile.

**Beef Empanadas**

Dough Ingredients:

- 3 cups all-purpose flour
- 1 teaspoon salt
- 1/2 cup unsalted butter, cold and cut into cubes
- 1 large egg
- 1/2 cup cold water
- 1 tablespoon white vinegar

Filling Ingredients:

- 1 tablespoon olive oil
- 1 small onion, finely chopped
- 2 cloves garlic, minced
- 1 pound ground beef
- 1 teaspoon ground cumin
- 1 teaspoon paprika
- 1/2 teaspoon dried oregano
- Salt and pepper to taste
- 1/2 cup green olives, pitted and chopped (optional)
- 2 hard-boiled eggs, chopped (optional)
- 1/4 cup raisins (optional)

Egg Wash:

- 1 egg, beaten
- 1 tablespoon water

Instructions:

1. Prepare the Dough:

   In a large mixing bowl, combine the flour and salt. Cut in the cold butter using a pastry cutter or fork until the mixture resembles coarse crumbs.

   In a small bowl, whisk together the egg, cold water, and vinegar. Gradually add the wet ingredients to the flour mixture, stirring until the dough comes together.

   Turn the dough out onto a lightly floured surface and knead gently until smooth. Wrap the dough in plastic wrap and refrigerate for at least 30 minutes while you prepare the filling.

2. Prepare the Filling:

Heat olive oil in a large skillet over medium heat. Add the chopped onion and garlic, and sauté until softened and fragrant, about 2-3 minutes.

Add the ground beef to the skillet, breaking it up with a spoon. Cook until browned and cooked through, stirring occasionally.

Stir in the ground cumin, paprika, dried oregano, salt, and pepper, cooking for another 1-2 minutes to toast the spices.

Remove the skillet from the heat and let the beef mixture cool slightly. Stir in the chopped olives, hard-boiled eggs, and raisins if using. Set aside to cool completely.

3. Assemble the Empanadas:

Preheat the oven to 375°F (190°C) and line a baking sheet with parchment paper.

On a lightly floured surface, roll out the chilled dough to about 1/8 inch thickness. Use a round cutter or a small bowl to cut out circles of dough, approximately 4-5 inches in diameter.

Place a spoonful of the beef filling in the center of each dough circle. Fold the dough over the filling to form a half-moon shape, then crimp the edges with a fork to seal. Repeat with the remaining dough and filling.

Transfer the assembled empanadas to the prepared baking sheet, leaving some space between each one.

4. Bake the Empanadas:

In a small bowl, whisk together the egg and water to make the egg wash. Brush the tops of the empanadas with the egg wash.

Bake in the preheated oven for 20-25 minutes, or until the empanadas are golden brown and crispy.

Remove from the oven and let cool slightly before serving. Enjoy the beef empanadas warm or at room temperature, optionally with chimichurri sauce or salsa on the side.

These beef empanadas are delicious as appetizers, snacks, or even as a main course served with a side salad. Feel free to customize the filling with your favorite ingredients, and experiment with different spices to suit your taste preferences.

# Mini Crab and Corn Fritters

Ingredients:

- 1 cup lump crab meat, drained and picked over for shells
- 1 cup fresh or frozen corn kernels
- 1/4 cup finely chopped red bell pepper
- 2 green onions, finely chopped
- 1/4 cup chopped fresh cilantro or parsley
- 1/2 cup all-purpose flour
- 1 teaspoon baking powder
- 1/2 teaspoon salt
- 1/4 teaspoon black pepper
- 2 large eggs
- 1/4 cup milk
- Vegetable oil, for frying
- Lemon wedges, for serving (optional)
- Tartar sauce or remoulade sauce, for dipping (optional)

Instructions:

Prepare the Ingredients:
- If using frozen corn, thaw it and pat it dry with paper towels to remove excess moisture.
- Drain the lump crab meat and pick through it to remove any shells or cartilage. Flake the crab meat into smaller pieces if necessary.
- Finely chop the red bell pepper, green onions, and fresh cilantro or parsley.

Make the Batter:
- In a large mixing bowl, combine the crab meat, corn kernels, chopped red bell pepper, green onions, and chopped cilantro or parsley.
- In a separate bowl, whisk together the flour, baking powder, salt, and black pepper.
- In another bowl, whisk together the eggs and milk until well combined.
- Gradually add the dry ingredients to the wet ingredients, stirring until a smooth batter forms.
- Pour the batter over the crab and corn mixture, stirring until everything is evenly coated.

Fry the Fritters:
- In a large skillet or frying pan, heat vegetable oil over medium-high heat until hot but not smoking.
- Drop spoonfuls of the fritter batter into the hot oil, using about 1-2 tablespoons of batter for each fritter. Flatten slightly with the back of the spoon.
- Cook the fritters in batches, being careful not to overcrowd the pan, until golden brown and crispy on both sides, about 2-3 minutes per side.

- Use a slotted spoon to transfer the cooked fritters to a paper towel-lined plate to drain excess oil.

Serve:
- Serve the mini crab and corn fritters hot, garnished with fresh cilantro or parsley and lemon wedges if desired.
- Optionally, serve with tartar sauce or remoulade sauce on the side for dipping.

Enjoy these delicious mini crab and corn fritters as a tasty appetizer or snack. They're sure to be a hit at any party or gathering!

**Antipasto Skewers with Salami, Cheese, and Olives**

Ingredients:

- Thinly sliced salami
- Cherry or grape tomatoes
- Fresh mozzarella balls (bocconcini)
- Kalamata or green olives, pitted
- Marinated artichoke hearts, drained and halved
- Marinated or roasted red bell peppers, cut into bite-sized pieces
- Wooden or bamboo skewers

Instructions:

Prepare Ingredients:
- If using wooden or bamboo skewers, soak them in water for about 30 minutes to prevent them from burning while grilling or broiling.
- Slice the salami into bite-sized pieces, if not already sliced.
- Drain any excess liquid from the marinated artichoke hearts and roasted red bell peppers.

Assemble Skewers:
- Begin by threading a piece of salami onto the skewer, folding or bunching it up slightly for a decorative effect.
- Follow the salami with a cherry or grape tomato, then a mozzarella ball (bocconcini), and alternate with olives, artichoke hearts, and roasted red bell peppers, threading them onto the skewer in any order you prefer.
- Continue to thread the ingredients onto the skewers until each skewer is filled, leaving a little space at the end for easy handling.

Arrange and Serve:
- Once all the skewers are assembled, arrange them on a serving platter or plate.
- Optionally, drizzle the skewers with a bit of extra-virgin olive oil and sprinkle with freshly ground black pepper or chopped fresh herbs like basil or parsley for extra flavor and presentation.
- Serve the antipasto skewers immediately, or cover and refrigerate until ready to serve.

These antipasto skewers are not only delicious but also easy to customize based on your preferences. Feel free to add other antipasto ingredients such as marinated mushrooms, chunks of Italian cheeses like provolone or Asiago, or slices of cured meats like prosciutto or soppressata. Enjoy these flavorful skewers as a tasty appetizer or snack at your next gathering!

**Coconut Shrimp with Mango Dipping Sauce**

Ingredients:

For the Coconut Shrimp:

- 1 pound large shrimp, peeled and deveined (tails left on or removed, as desired)
- 1 cup sweetened shredded coconut
- 1 cup Panko breadcrumbs
- 1/2 cup all-purpose flour
- 2 large eggs
- 1/2 teaspoon salt
- 1/4 teaspoon black pepper
- Vegetable oil, for frying

For the Mango Dipping Sauce:

- 1 ripe mango, peeled and diced
- 1/4 cup mayonnaise
- 2 tablespoons honey
- 1 tablespoon Dijon mustard
- 1 tablespoon lime juice
- 1 teaspoon Sriracha sauce (optional, for heat)
- Salt and pepper to taste

For Garnish (optional):

- Fresh cilantro or parsley, chopped
- Lime wedges

Instructions:

1. Prepare the Mango Dipping Sauce:

> In a blender or food processor, combine the diced mango, mayonnaise, honey, Dijon mustard, lime juice, and Sriracha sauce (if using).
> Blend until smooth and creamy. Season with salt and pepper to taste. Transfer the sauce to a serving bowl and set aside.

2. Prepare the Coconut Shrimp:

In three separate shallow bowls, set up your breading station. In one bowl, place the flour. In another bowl, beat the eggs. In the third bowl, combine the sweetened shredded coconut and Panko breadcrumbs.

Season the shrimp with salt and pepper.

Dip each shrimp first in the flour, shaking off any excess, then in the beaten eggs, and finally coat it thoroughly in the coconut-Panko mixture, pressing gently to adhere.

Place the coated shrimp on a baking sheet lined with parchment paper and chill in the refrigerator for about 15-20 minutes. Chilling helps the coating adhere better during frying.

In a large skillet or deep fryer, heat vegetable oil to 350°F (180°C).

Fry the coconut shrimp in batches until golden brown and crispy, about 2-3 minutes per side. Be careful not to overcrowd the pan.

Once cooked, transfer the shrimp to a paper towel-lined plate to drain excess oil.

3. Serve:

Arrange the coconut shrimp on a serving platter.

Garnish with chopped fresh cilantro or parsley and serve with lime wedges alongside the mango dipping sauce.

Enjoy your coconut shrimp with mango dipping sauce as a delicious appetizer or main dish!

These coconut shrimp are crispy on the outside, tender on the inside, and the mango dipping sauce adds a burst of tropical flavor. It's a perfect combination that will surely impress your guests or family.

**Mini Tacos with Guacamole**

Ingredients:

For the Mini Tacos:

- 12 small taco shells or mini tortillas
- 1 cup cooked and seasoned protein of your choice (such as seasoned ground beef, shredded chicken, or grilled shrimp)
- 1 cup shredded lettuce
- 1/2 cup diced tomatoes
- 1/2 cup shredded cheese (such as cheddar or Monterey Jack)
- 1/4 cup diced red onion (optional)
- 1/4 cup chopped fresh cilantro (optional)
- Lime wedges, for serving (optional)

For the Guacamole:

- 2 ripe avocados
- 1 small tomato, diced
- 1/4 cup diced red onion
- 1 clove garlic, minced
- 2 tablespoons chopped fresh cilantro
- Juice of 1 lime
- Salt and pepper to taste

Instructions:

1. Prepare the Guacamole:

   Cut the avocados in half, remove the pits, and scoop the flesh into a mixing bowl.
   Mash the avocados with a fork until desired consistency is reached.
   Add the diced tomato, red onion, minced garlic, chopped cilantro, lime juice, salt, and pepper to the mashed avocado. Stir until well combined.
   Taste and adjust seasonings as needed. Cover the guacamole with plastic wrap, pressing it down onto the surface to prevent browning, and refrigerate until ready to use.

2. Assemble the Mini Tacos:

   Preheat your oven according to the instructions on the taco shell or mini tortilla package.
   Warm the taco shells or mini tortillas in the oven as directed.

Once warmed, fill each taco shell or mini tortilla with a spoonful of cooked and seasoned protein of your choice.

Top each mini taco with shredded lettuce, diced tomatoes, shredded cheese, diced red onion (if using), and chopped fresh cilantro (if using).

Serve the mini tacos with lime wedges and the prepared guacamole on the side for dipping or topping.

3. Serve:

Arrange the mini tacos on a serving platter.

Serve immediately, allowing guests to add guacamole as desired.

Enjoy your delicious mini tacos with guacamole as a tasty appetizer or snack!

Feel free to customize the mini tacos with your favorite toppings and protein choices. You can also add sour cream, salsa, or hot sauce for additional flavor. These mini tacos are sure to be a hit at your next party or gathering!

**Bacon-Wrapped Scallops**

Ingredients:

- 12 large sea scallops, patted dry
- 12 slices of bacon, cut in half
- Salt and pepper, to taste
- Toothpicks, for securing

Optional Glaze (for extra flavor):

- 1/4 cup maple syrup
- 1 tablespoon soy sauce
- 1 teaspoon Dijon mustard
- 1 clove garlic, minced
- Pinch of black pepper

Instructions:

1. Preheat the oven:

- Preheat your oven to 400°F (200°C). Line a baking sheet with aluminum foil and place a wire rack on top. This helps the bacon cook evenly and prevents it from getting soggy.

2. Prepare the scallops:

   Season the scallops with salt and pepper to taste.
   Wrap each scallop with a half-slice of bacon, securing it with a toothpick. Make sure the bacon wraps around the scallop tightly.

3. Optional glaze:

- If using the glaze, whisk together the maple syrup, soy sauce, Dijon mustard, minced garlic, and black pepper in a small bowl.

4. Glaze the scallops:

- Brush each bacon-wrapped scallop with the glaze mixture if desired. This adds extra flavor and caramelization to the bacon.

5. Bake:

- Place the bacon-wrapped scallops on the wire rack on the prepared baking sheet.
- Bake in the preheated oven for 15-20 minutes or until the bacon is crispy and the scallops are cooked through. The internal temperature of the scallops should reach 120°F (49°C).
- If you like your bacon extra crispy, you can broil the scallops for an additional 1-2 minutes at the end of cooking.

6. Serve:

- Remove the toothpicks from the bacon-wrapped scallops before serving.
- Optionally, garnish with chopped parsley or green onions for a pop of color.
- Serve the bacon-wrapped scallops hot as an appetizer or main dish, accompanied by your favorite dipping sauce such as aioli or cocktail sauce.

Enjoy these bacon-wrapped scallops as a delicious appetizer for your next dinner party or special occasion. They're sure to impress your guests with their combination of flavors and textures.

**Greek Yogurt and Cucumber Canapés**

Ingredients:

- 1 large cucumber
- 1 cup Greek yogurt
- 1 tablespoon fresh dill, chopped
- 1 tablespoon fresh mint, chopped
- 1 clove garlic, minced
- 1 teaspoon lemon juice
- Salt and pepper to taste
- Sliced bread or crackers, for serving

Optional Garnishes:

- Cherry tomatoes, halved
- Kalamata olives, pitted and chopped
- Crumbled feta cheese
- Extra chopped fresh herbs

Instructions:

1. Prepare the Cucumber:

   Peel the cucumber if desired, then slice it thinly into rounds. Alternatively, you can leave the peel on for added texture and color.
   Place the cucumber slices on a paper towel-lined plate to absorb excess moisture while you prepare the yogurt mixture.

2. Make the Yogurt Mixture:

   In a mixing bowl, combine the Greek yogurt, chopped fresh dill, chopped fresh mint, minced garlic, and lemon juice.
   Season the mixture with salt and pepper to taste. Stir until well combined.

3. Assemble the Canapés:

   Arrange the sliced bread or crackers on a serving platter.
   Spoon a small dollop of the yogurt mixture onto each slice of bread or cracker.
   Top each yogurt-topped bread or cracker with a cucumber slice.
   Optionally, garnish each canapé with halved cherry tomatoes, chopped Kalamata olives, crumbled feta cheese, or extra chopped fresh herbs for added flavor and visual appeal.

4. Serve:

      Arrange the Greek yogurt and cucumber canapés on a serving platter.
      Serve immediately as a light and refreshing appetizer or snack.

These Greek yogurt and cucumber canapés are not only delicious but also healthy and easy to make. They're perfect for serving at parties, brunches, or any occasion where you want to impress your guests with a tasty and elegant appetizer. Enjoy!

**Pigs in a Blanket with Mustard Dip**

Ingredients:

For the Pigs in a Blanket:

- 1 package cocktail sausages or mini hot dogs
- 1 package crescent roll dough or puff pastry
- 1 egg, beaten (for egg wash)
- Sesame seeds or poppy seeds (optional, for garnish)

For the Mustard Dip:

- 1/2 cup mayonnaise
- 2 tablespoons Dijon mustard
- 1 tablespoon honey
- 1 tablespoon lemon juice
- Salt and pepper to taste

Instructions:

1. Preheat the Oven:

- Preheat your oven to the temperature specified on the crescent roll dough or puff pastry package.

2. Prepare the Pigs in a Blanket:

If using crescent roll dough, separate it into triangles along the perforated lines. If using puff pastry, roll it out slightly and cut it into strips.
Place a cocktail sausage or mini hot dog at the wider end of each crescent roll triangle or puff pastry strip.
Roll up the dough around the sausage, starting from the wider end, and place it seam-side down on a baking sheet lined with parchment paper.
Repeat with the remaining sausages and dough.
Brush the tops of the wrapped sausages with beaten egg and sprinkle with sesame seeds or poppy seeds if desired.

3. Bake:

- Bake the pigs in a blanket in the preheated oven according to the instructions on the crescent roll dough or puff pastry package, or until golden brown and cooked through.

4. Make the Mustard Dip:

In a small bowl, whisk together the mayonnaise, Dijon mustard, honey, and lemon juice until smooth.
Season with salt and pepper to taste. Adjust the ingredients to achieve the desired flavor and consistency.

5. Serve:

- Arrange the pigs in a blanket on a serving platter alongside the mustard dip.
- Serve hot, allowing guests to dip the pigs in a blanket into the mustard dip.

These pigs in a blanket with mustard dip are sure to be a hit at your next gathering. They're quick to make, fun to eat, and bursting with flavor. Enjoy!

**Mini Falafel with Tahini Sauce**

Ingredients:

For the Mini Falafel:

- 1 can (15 ounces) chickpeas, drained and rinsed
- 1/4 cup chopped fresh parsley
- 1/4 cup chopped fresh cilantro
- 1/4 cup chopped onion
- 2 cloves garlic, minced
- 1 teaspoon ground cumin
- 1 teaspoon ground coriander
- 1/2 teaspoon salt
- 1/4 teaspoon black pepper
- 2 tablespoons all-purpose flour or chickpea flour (for a gluten-free option)
- Vegetable oil, for frying

For the Tahini Sauce:

- 1/4 cup tahini (sesame seed paste)
- 2 tablespoons lemon juice
- 1 clove garlic, minced
- 2-4 tablespoons water, as needed
- Salt, to taste
- Chopped fresh parsley or cilantro, for garnish (optional)

Instructions:

1. Prepare the Mini Falafel:

In a food processor, combine the drained and rinsed chickpeas, chopped parsley, chopped cilantro, chopped onion, minced garlic, ground cumin, ground coriander, salt, pepper, and flour.
Pulse the mixture until everything is well combined and the chickpeas are finely chopped but not pureed. You want some texture remaining.
Transfer the falafel mixture to a bowl and let it rest in the refrigerator for at least 30 minutes. This helps the mixture firm up and makes it easier to shape.

2. Shape and Fry the Falafel:

Heat vegetable oil in a frying pan over medium heat.

While the oil is heating, shape the falafel mixture into small balls or patties, about 1 tablespoon each.

Once the oil is hot, carefully place the falafel in the pan in batches, ensuring they are not overcrowded. Fry until golden brown and crispy on all sides, about 2-3 minutes per side.

Use a slotted spoon to transfer the cooked falafel to a paper towel-lined plate to drain excess oil.

## 3. Make the Tahini Sauce:

In a small bowl, whisk together the tahini, lemon juice, minced garlic, and salt. Gradually add water, 1 tablespoon at a time, whisking continuously until you reach the desired consistency. The sauce should be smooth and pourable but not too runny.

Taste and adjust the seasoning, adding more salt or lemon juice if needed.

## 4. Serve:

- Arrange the mini falafel on a serving platter.
- Drizzle the tahini sauce over the falafel or serve it on the side for dipping.
- Garnish with chopped fresh parsley or cilantro if desired.
- Serve the mini falafel with tahini sauce warm or at room temperature.

These mini falafel with tahini sauce are flavorful, crunchy on the outside, and tender on the inside. They make a fantastic appetizer or snack that's sure to please a crowd. Enjoy!

**Chicken Quesadilla Triangles with Salsa**

Ingredients:

For the Chicken Quesadilla:

- 2 cups cooked chicken breast, shredded or diced
- 1 cup shredded cheese (cheddar, Monterey Jack, or a blend)
- 1/2 cup diced bell peppers (any color)
- 1/4 cup diced red onion
- 1/4 cup chopped fresh cilantro
- 1 teaspoon chili powder
- 1/2 teaspoon ground cumin
- Salt and pepper to taste
- 6 medium-sized flour tortillas
- Cooking spray or olive oil

For Serving:

- Salsa (store-bought or homemade)
- Sour cream
- Guacamole or diced avocado

Instructions:

1. Prepare the Chicken Quesadilla Filling:

   In a mixing bowl, combine the cooked chicken breast, shredded cheese, diced bell peppers, diced red onion, chopped fresh cilantro, chili powder, ground cumin, salt, and pepper. Mix until well combined.

2. Assemble the Quesadillas:

   Lay a flour tortilla flat on a clean surface.
   Spread a portion of the chicken filling evenly over half of the tortilla, leaving a small border around the edges.
   Fold the empty half of the tortilla over the filling to create a half-moon shape.

3. Cook the Quesadillas:

   Preheat a large skillet or griddle over medium heat.
   Lightly spray the skillet or griddle with cooking spray or brush with olive oil.

Place the folded quesadillas in the skillet or griddle and cook for 2-3 minutes on each side, or until golden brown and crispy, and the cheese is melted.
Repeat the process with the remaining quesadillas, working in batches if necessary.

## 4. Cut into Triangles:

Once cooked, transfer the quesadillas to a cutting board and let them cool for a minute.
Use a sharp knife to cut each quesadilla into triangles.

## 5. Serve:

Arrange the chicken quesadilla triangles on a serving platter.
Serve with salsa, sour cream, and guacamole or diced avocado on the side for dipping.
Garnish with additional chopped cilantro, if desired.

These chicken quesadilla triangles with salsa are perfect for serving as appetizers at parties or as a tasty snack for any occasion. They're flavorful, satisfying, and easy to customize with your favorite toppings. Enjoy!

**Mushroom and Gruyere Tartlets**

Ingredients:

For the Tartlet Shells:

- 1 package (about 14 ounces) pre-made puff pastry, thawed if frozen
- All-purpose flour, for dusting

For the Mushroom Filling:

- 1 tablespoon olive oil
- 1 tablespoon unsalted butter
- 8 ounces mushrooms (such as cremini or button), finely chopped
- 2 cloves garlic, minced
- 2 tablespoons chopped fresh thyme
- Salt and pepper to taste

For the Gruyere Cheese Mixture:

- 1 cup shredded Gruyere cheese
- 1/4 cup grated Parmesan cheese
- 1/4 cup sour cream
- 1/4 cup mayonnaise
- 1 tablespoon Dijon mustard
- 1/4 teaspoon garlic powder
- Salt and pepper to taste

Optional Garnish:

- Fresh thyme leaves
- Chopped chives

Instructions:

1. Preheat the Oven:

   Preheat your oven to 375°F (190°C).
   Lightly grease a mini muffin tin with butter or non-stick cooking spray.

2. Prepare the Tartlet Shells:

   On a lightly floured surface, roll out the puff pastry to about 1/8 inch thickness.

Using a round cookie cutter or a small glass, cut out circles of puff pastry slightly larger than the wells of the mini muffin tin.

Gently press each puff pastry circle into the wells of the mini muffin tin, forming small tartlet shells.

Prick the bottoms of the tartlet shells with a fork to prevent puffing during baking.

Bake the tartlet shells in the preheated oven for about 10-12 minutes, or until lightly golden. Remove from the oven and set aside.

3. Prepare the Mushroom Filling:

Heat olive oil and butter in a skillet over medium heat.

Add the finely chopped mushrooms to the skillet and cook, stirring occasionally, until they release their moisture and become golden brown, about 5-7 minutes.

Add the minced garlic and chopped fresh thyme to the skillet and cook for an additional 1-2 minutes.

Season the mushroom mixture with salt and pepper to taste. Remove from heat and set aside to cool slightly.

4. Make the Gruyere Cheese Mixture:

In a mixing bowl, combine the shredded Gruyere cheese, grated Parmesan cheese, sour cream, mayonnaise, Dijon mustard, garlic powder, salt, and pepper. Stir until well combined.

5. Assemble and Bake the Tartlets:

Spoon a small amount of the mushroom filling into each pre-baked tartlet shell, filling them about halfway.

Top each tartlet with a spoonful of the Gruyere cheese mixture, covering the mushrooms.

Return the filled tartlets to the oven and bake for an additional 10-12 minutes, or until the cheese mixture is bubbly and lightly golden.

Remove from the oven and let the tartlets cool slightly before serving.

6. Serve:

Garnish the mushroom and Gruyere tartlets with fresh thyme leaves or chopped chives, if desired.

Serve warm as a delightful appetizer or snack.

These mushroom and Gruyere tartlets are sure to impress your guests with their savory flavors and flaky pastry. Enjoy!

**Thai Chicken Lettuce Wraps**

Ingredients:

For the Chicken Filling:

- 1 lb (450g) ground chicken or chicken breast, finely chopped
- 2 tablespoons vegetable oil
- 3 cloves garlic, minced
- 1 small onion, finely chopped
- 1 red bell pepper, finely chopped
- 1 carrot, grated
- 1/4 cup soy sauce or tamari (for gluten-free option)
- 2 tablespoons oyster sauce
- 1 tablespoon fish sauce
- 1 tablespoon brown sugar or honey
- 1 teaspoon sesame oil
- 1 teaspoon freshly grated ginger
- 1/4 teaspoon red pepper flakes (optional, for heat)
- Salt and pepper to taste
- 1/4 cup chopped fresh cilantro or Thai basil
- 1/4 cup chopped peanuts (optional, for garnish)
- Lime wedges, for serving

For Serving:

- Large lettuce leaves (such as butter or iceberg lettuce)
- Thinly sliced cucumber
- Thinly sliced red onion
- Chopped fresh cilantro or Thai basil
- Sriracha or chili garlic sauce (optional, for extra heat)

Instructions:

1. Prepare the Chicken Filling:

   Heat vegetable oil in a large skillet or wok over medium-high heat.
   Add minced garlic and chopped onion to the skillet and cook until fragrant, about 1-2 minutes.
   Add ground chicken (or chopped chicken breast) to the skillet and cook, breaking it apart with a spoon, until it's no longer pink and begins to brown.

Stir in the finely chopped red bell pepper and grated carrot, and cook for another 2-3 minutes until the vegetables are tender.

In a small bowl, whisk together soy sauce (or tamari), oyster sauce, fish sauce, brown sugar (or honey), sesame oil, grated ginger, and red pepper flakes if using. Pour the sauce mixture over the chicken and vegetables in the skillet.

Stir well to combine and let the mixture simmer for a few more minutes until the sauce thickens slightly.

Season with salt and pepper to taste. Stir in chopped fresh cilantro or Thai basil.

## 2. Assemble the Lettuce Wraps:

Arrange the large lettuce leaves on a serving platter.

Spoon the chicken filling into the center of each lettuce leaf.

Top with thinly sliced cucumber, red onion, and additional chopped cilantro or Thai basil.

Optionally, garnish with chopped peanuts for added crunch.

Serve the Thai chicken lettuce wraps with lime wedges and Sriracha or chili garlic sauce on the side for extra flavor.

## 3. Enjoy:

- To eat, simply fold the lettuce leaf around the filling like a taco and enjoy!

These Thai chicken lettuce wraps are fresh, flavorful, and perfect for a light meal or appetizer. They're also customizable, so feel free to add your favorite toppings or adjust the seasoning to suit your taste preferences. Enjoy!

**Mini Beef Sliders with Caramelized Onions**

Ingredients:

For the Beef Patties:

- 1 pound ground beef (preferably 80/20 for juiciness)
- Salt and pepper to taste
- 1 teaspoon garlic powder
- 1 teaspoon onion powder
- 1 tablespoon Worcestershire sauce
- Slider buns or dinner rolls

For the Caramelized Onions:

- 2 large onions, thinly sliced
- 2 tablespoons butter
- 1 tablespoon olive oil
- Salt and pepper to taste
- 1 tablespoon brown sugar (optional, for added sweetness)

Optional Toppings:

- Sliced cheese (such as cheddar or Swiss)
- Lettuce leaves
- Sliced tomatoes
- Pickles
- Ketchup, mustard, or mayonnaise

Instructions:

1. Prepare the Beef Patties:

   In a mixing bowl, combine the ground beef, salt, pepper, garlic powder, onion powder, and Worcestershire sauce. Mix until well combined.
   Divide the beef mixture into small portions and shape them into mini patties, slightly larger than the size of your slider buns.
   Make a slight indentation in the center of each patty with your thumb to prevent them from puffing up while cooking.

2. Caramelize the Onions:

   Heat butter and olive oil in a large skillet over medium-low heat.

Add the thinly sliced onions to the skillet and cook, stirring occasionally, until they become soft and golden brown, about 20-30 minutes.

If desired, sprinkle brown sugar over the onions to help caramelize them further.

Continue cooking until the onions are deeply caramelized and sweet. Season with salt and pepper to taste.

## 3. Cook the Beef Patties:

Heat a grill pan or skillet over medium-high heat.

Cook the beef patties for 2-3 minutes per side, or until they reach your desired level of doneness. If adding cheese, place a slice on top of each patty during the last minute of cooking to melt.

Once cooked, transfer the beef patties to a plate and let them rest for a few minutes.

## 4. Assemble the Sliders:

Slice the slider buns or dinner rolls in half horizontally.

Place a beef patty on the bottom half of each bun.

Top each patty with a spoonful of caramelized onions.

Add any optional toppings such as lettuce, tomato slices, pickles, ketchup, mustard, or mayonnaise.

Place the top half of the bun on top of each slider.

## 5. Serve:

- Arrange the mini beef sliders on a platter and serve immediately. Enjoy your delicious sliders as a tasty appetizer or snack!

These mini beef sliders with caramelized onions are sure to be a hit at your next gathering.

They're flavorful, juicy, and perfect for any occasion. Enjoy!

**Cranberry and Brie Phyllo Cups**

Ingredients:

- 1 package (15 count) mini phyllo pastry shells
- 4 ounces Brie cheese, rind removed, cut into small cubes
- 1/2 cup cranberry sauce (homemade or store-bought)
- Fresh thyme leaves or chopped parsley, for garnish (optional)

Instructions:

1. Preheat the Oven:

- Preheat your oven to 350°F (175°C).

2. Assemble the Phyllo Cups:

Place the mini phyllo pastry shells on a baking sheet lined with parchment paper or aluminum foil for easy cleanup.
Place a small cube of Brie cheese into the bottom of each phyllo pastry shell.

3. Add Cranberry Sauce:

Spoon a small dollop of cranberry sauce on top of the Brie cheese in each phyllo cup. You can adjust the amount of cranberry sauce based on your preference for sweetness. If desired, garnish each phyllo cup with a few fresh thyme leaves or chopped parsley for color and flavor.

4. Bake:

- Place the filled phyllo cups in the preheated oven and bake for 5-7 minutes, or until the Brie cheese is melted and bubbly, and the phyllo pastry is golden brown and crispy.

5. Serve:

- Remove the baked cranberry and Brie phyllo cups from the oven and let them cool slightly before serving.
- Arrange them on a serving platter and serve warm as a delicious appetizer or snack.

These cranberry and Brie phyllo cups are sure to impress your guests with their combination of sweet and savory flavors and elegant presentation. They're perfect for holiday gatherings, cocktail parties, or any occasion where you want to serve a tasty and easy-to-make appetizer. Enjoy!

**Teriyaki Glazed Meatball Skewers**

Ingredients:

For the Meatballs:

- 1 pound ground beef or ground chicken
- 1/2 cup breadcrumbs
- 1/4 cup finely chopped onion
- 1 clove garlic, minced
- 1 egg
- 2 tablespoons soy sauce
- 1 tablespoon Worcestershire sauce
- Salt and pepper to taste
- Vegetable oil, for cooking

For the Teriyaki Glaze:

- 1/2 cup soy sauce
- 1/4 cup water
- 2 tablespoons honey or brown sugar
- 1 tablespoon rice vinegar
- 1 clove garlic, minced
- 1 teaspoon grated ginger
- 1 tablespoon cornstarch mixed with 2 tablespoons water (optional, for thickening)

For Serving:

- Sesame seeds, for garnish (optional)
- Sliced green onions, for garnish (optional)

Equipment:

- Wooden or metal skewers, soaked in water if wooden

Instructions:

1. Prepare the Meatballs:

In a large mixing bowl, combine the ground beef or chicken, breadcrumbs, finely chopped onion, minced garlic, egg, soy sauce, Worcestershire sauce, salt, and pepper. Mix until well combined.
Shape the mixture into small meatballs, about 1 inch in diameter.

2. Cook the Meatballs:

> Heat a bit of vegetable oil in a skillet over medium heat.
> Add the meatballs to the skillet in batches, making sure not to overcrowd the pan.
> Cook the meatballs for 8-10 minutes, turning occasionally, until they are browned on all sides and cooked through. Remove from the skillet and set aside.

3. Make the Teriyaki Glaze:

> In a small saucepan, combine the soy sauce, water, honey or brown sugar, rice vinegar, minced garlic, and grated ginger.
> Bring the mixture to a simmer over medium heat, stirring occasionally.
> If you prefer a thicker glaze, whisk in the cornstarch mixture and continue to simmer until the sauce thickens slightly.

4. Glaze the Meatballs:

> Thread the cooked meatballs onto the skewers, leaving a bit of space between each one.
> Brush the teriyaki glaze generously over the meatballs, coating them evenly.
> Reserve some of the glaze for serving.

5. Grill or Broil:

> Preheat your grill or broiler to medium-high heat.
> Place the skewers on the grill or under the broiler and cook for 2-3 minutes on each side, or until the glaze is caramelized and the meatballs are heated through.

6. Serve:

> Transfer the teriyaki glazed meatball skewers to a serving platter.
> Garnish with sesame seeds and sliced green onions, if desired.
> Serve hot with the reserved teriyaki glaze on the side for dipping.

These teriyaki glazed meatball skewers are perfect for serving as appetizers at parties or as a flavorful main dish. Enjoy the sweet and savory combination of flavors!

**Spinach and Artichoke Stuffed Phyllo Cups**

Ingredients:

For the Spinach and Artichoke Filling:

- 1 tablespoon olive oil
- 2 cloves garlic, minced
- 1 (10-ounce) package frozen chopped spinach, thawed and squeezed dry
- 1 (14-ounce) can artichoke hearts, drained and chopped
- 4 ounces cream cheese, softened
- 1/2 cup sour cream
- 1/4 cup mayonnaise
- 1/2 cup shredded mozzarella cheese
- 1/4 cup grated Parmesan cheese
- Salt and pepper to taste

For the Phyllo Cups:

- 1 package mini phyllo pastry shells (15-count)
- Cooking spray or melted butter

Optional Garnish:

- Chopped fresh parsley or chives
- Grated Parmesan cheese

Instructions:

1. Prepare the Spinach and Artichoke Filling:

Heat olive oil in a skillet over medium heat. Add minced garlic and cook for 1 minute until fragrant.
Add thawed and squeezed dry chopped spinach to the skillet. Cook for 2-3 minutes, stirring occasionally.
Stir in chopped artichoke hearts and cook for an additional 2 minutes.
In a mixing bowl, combine the cooked spinach and artichoke mixture with softened cream cheese, sour cream, mayonnaise, shredded mozzarella cheese, and grated Parmesan cheese. Mix until well combined. Season with salt and pepper to taste.

2. Preheat the Oven:

- Preheat your oven to 350°F (175°C).

3. Assemble the Phyllo Cups:

Arrange the mini phyllo pastry shells on a baking sheet lined with parchment paper.
Fill each phyllo pastry shell with a spoonful of the spinach and artichoke filling, dividing it evenly among the cups.

4. Bake:

- Place the filled phyllo cups in the preheated oven and bake for 10-12 minutes, or until the filling is heated through and the phyllo pastry is golden brown and crispy.

5. Garnish and Serve:

- Remove the spinach and artichoke stuffed phyllo cups from the oven and let them cool slightly.
- Garnish with chopped fresh parsley or chives and grated Parmesan cheese, if desired.
- Serve warm as a delicious appetizer at your next party or gathering.

These spinach and artichoke stuffed phyllo cups are sure to be a hit with your guests. They're creamy, flavorful, and perfectly crispy, making them an irresistible appetizer option. Enjoy!

**BBQ Pulled Pork Sliders**

Ingredients:

For the Pulled Pork:

- 2-3 pounds pork shoulder or pork butt
- Salt and pepper to taste
- 1 tablespoon olive oil
- 1 onion, chopped
- 3 cloves garlic, minced
- 1 cup barbecue sauce (homemade or store-bought)
- 1 cup chicken or vegetable broth
- 1/4 cup apple cider vinegar
- 2 tablespoons brown sugar
- 1 teaspoon smoked paprika
- 1/2 teaspoon garlic powder
- 1/2 teaspoon onion powder
- 1/4 teaspoon cayenne pepper (optional, for heat)

For Serving:

- Slider buns
- Coleslaw (optional, for topping)
- Pickles (optional, for topping)

Instructions:

1. Prepare the Pulled Pork:

Season the pork shoulder or pork butt generously with salt and pepper.
Heat olive oil in a large skillet or Dutch oven over medium-high heat. Add the seasoned pork and sear on all sides until browned, about 3-4 minutes per side.
Transfer the seared pork to a slow cooker.
In the same skillet or Dutch oven, add chopped onion and minced garlic. Cook until softened, about 3-4 minutes.
Add barbecue sauce, chicken or vegetable broth, apple cider vinegar, brown sugar, smoked paprika, garlic powder, onion powder, and cayenne pepper (if using) to the skillet or Dutch oven. Stir to combine and bring the mixture to a simmer.
Pour the barbecue sauce mixture over the pork in the slow cooker.
Cover and cook on low heat for 6-8 hours or on high heat for 4-5 hours, or until the pork is tender and easily shreds with a fork.

2. Shred the Pork:

   Once the pork is cooked, remove it from the slow cooker and transfer it to a cutting board or large plate.
   Use two forks to shred the pork into bite-sized pieces. Discard any excess fat.

3. Assemble the Sliders:

   Split the slider buns and lightly toast them if desired.
   Place a spoonful of pulled pork onto the bottom half of each slider bun.
   Top with coleslaw and pickles if desired.
   Place the top half of the slider bun on top of the filling to complete the sliders.

4. Serve:

   - Arrange the BBQ pulled pork sliders on a platter and serve warm. Enjoy!

These BBQ pulled pork sliders are perfect for parties, game days, or any casual gathering.

They're flavorful, tender, and sure to be a crowd-pleaser!

**Ceviche Shooters**

Ingredients:

For the Ceviche:

- 1 pound fresh white fish fillets (such as tilapia, snapper, or sea bass), diced into small cubes
- 1/2 pound shrimp, peeled, deveined, and diced into small pieces
- 1 cup fresh lime juice (about 8-10 limes)
- 1/2 cup fresh lemon juice (about 4-5 lemons)
- 1/2 cup fresh orange juice (about 2 oranges)
- 1/2 cup finely chopped red onion
- 1/2 cup diced cucumber
- 1/2 cup diced tomato, seeds removed
- 1/4 cup chopped cilantro
- 1 jalapeño pepper, seeded and finely chopped (optional)
- Salt and pepper to taste
- 1 avocado, diced (for garnish)

For Serving:

- Shot glasses or small glass cups
- Tortilla chips or plantain chips (optional)

Instructions:

1. Prepare the Seafood:

   In a large glass or ceramic bowl, combine the diced fish and shrimp.
   Pour the fresh lime juice, lemon juice, and orange juice over the seafood, making sure it's completely submerged.
   Cover the bowl with plastic wrap and refrigerate for about 30-60 minutes, or until the seafood is "cooked" in the acidic juices. The fish will turn opaque and firm when it's ready.

2. Assemble the Ceviche:

   Once the seafood is "cooked," drain off most of the citrus juices, leaving just a little to keep the ceviche moist.
   Add the finely chopped red onion, diced cucumber, diced tomato, chopped cilantro, and finely chopped jalapeño pepper (if using) to the bowl.

Season the ceviche with salt and pepper to taste. Gently toss everything together until well combined.

3. Serve in Shooters:

Using a small spoon, carefully transfer the ceviche mixture into shot glasses or small glass cups.
Top each ceviche shooter with diced avocado for garnish.
Optionally, serve each ceviche shooter with a small fork or spoon and a side of tortilla chips or plantain chips for dipping.

4. Serve Immediately:

- Serve the ceviche shooters immediately as a refreshing appetizer or amuse-bouche at your next gathering or party. Enjoy the burst of citrusy flavors and fresh seafood!

These ceviche shooters are not only delicious but also visually appealing and perfect for entertaining. Feel free to customize the recipe by adding your favorite ingredients such as mango, pineapple, or bell peppers. Enjoy the taste of the sea in every bite!

**Mini BLT Sandwiches**

Ingredients:

- Mini bread slices (such as cocktail bread or sliced baguette)
- Bacon slices, cooked until crispy
- Lettuce leaves, washed and dried
- Cherry or grape tomatoes, sliced
- Mayonnaise
- Toothpicks or cocktail picks

Instructions:

1. Prepare the Ingredients:

   Cook the bacon until crispy. Drain on paper towels and cut each strip into small pieces that will fit onto your mini bread slices.
   Wash and dry the lettuce leaves. Tear or cut them into smaller pieces to fit the size of your bread slices.
   Slice the cherry or grape tomatoes into thin rounds.

2. Assemble the Mini BLT Sandwiches:

   Lay out the mini bread slices on a clean work surface.
   Spread a thin layer of mayonnaise on each slice of bread.
   Place a piece of lettuce on half of the bread slices.
   Top the lettuce with a slice of tomato.
   Add a piece of crispy bacon on top of the tomato.
   Place the remaining bread slices on top to form sandwiches.

3. Secure with Toothpicks:

   Insert toothpicks or cocktail picks through the center of each mini sandwich to secure the layers together.

4. Serve:

- Arrange the mini BLT sandwiches on a serving platter or tray. Optionally, you can garnish the platter with additional lettuce leaves or cherry tomatoes.
- Serve immediately and enjoy!

These mini BLT sandwiches are perfect for parties, brunches, or any occasion where you want to serve a tasty and classic appetizer. They're easy to make and always a hit with guests. Enjoy the delicious combination of flavors!

**Stuffed Mini Bell Peppers with Cream Cheese and Bacon**

Ingredients:

- 12 mini bell peppers, halved and seeds removed
- 8 ounces cream cheese, softened
- 1/2 cup cooked bacon, crumbled
- 1/4 cup shredded cheddar cheese
- 2 green onions, thinly sliced
- 1 teaspoon garlic powder
- Salt and pepper to taste
- Chopped fresh parsley or chives for garnish (optional)

Instructions:

1. Preheat the Oven:

- Preheat your oven to 375°F (190°C). Line a baking sheet with parchment paper for easy cleanup.

2. Prepare the Bell Peppers:

- Slice each mini bell pepper in half lengthwise and remove the seeds and membranes. Rinse the peppers under cold water and pat dry with paper towels.

3. Make the Filling:

In a mixing bowl, combine the softened cream cheese, crumbled bacon, shredded cheddar cheese, sliced green onions, garlic powder, salt, and pepper. Mix until well combined.
Taste the mixture and adjust seasoning if necessary.

4. Stuff the Bell Peppers:

Spoon the cream cheese and bacon mixture into each halved bell pepper, filling them evenly.
Place the stuffed bell peppers on the prepared baking sheet, cut side up, in a single layer.

5. Bake:

- Bake the stuffed mini bell peppers in the preheated oven for 15-20 minutes, or until the peppers are tender and the filling is bubbly and lightly browned on top.

6. Serve:

- Remove the stuffed mini bell peppers from the oven and let them cool for a few minutes.
- Transfer the stuffed peppers to a serving platter and garnish with chopped fresh parsley or chives, if desired.
- Serve warm as a delicious appetizer or snack.

These stuffed mini bell peppers with cream cheese and bacon are sure to be a hit at your next gathering. They're creamy, savory, and packed with flavor, making them a perfect bite-sized treat for any occasion. Enjoy!

**Avocado Shrimp Cups**

Ingredients:

For the Shrimp:

- 1 pound large shrimp, peeled and deveined
- 1 tablespoon olive oil
- 2 cloves garlic, minced
- 1 teaspoon paprika
- 1/2 teaspoon cumin
- Salt and pepper to taste
- Juice of 1 lime

For the Avocado Mixture:

- 2 ripe avocados, peeled and diced
- 1/4 cup red onion, finely chopped
- 1/4 cup cherry tomatoes, diced
- 1/4 cup cilantro, chopped
- Juice of 1 lime
- Salt and pepper to taste

For Serving:

- 12 small tortillas (corn or flour)
- Cooking spray or olive oil
- Lime wedges for garnish
- Cilantro leaves for garnish

Instructions:

1. Prepare the Shrimp:

In a bowl, combine the peeled and deveined shrimp with olive oil, minced garlic, paprika, cumin, salt, pepper, and lime juice. Toss until the shrimp are well coated.
Heat a skillet over medium-high heat. Add the seasoned shrimp to the skillet and cook for 2-3 minutes per side, or until they are pink and cooked through. Remove from heat and set aside.

2. Make the Avocado Mixture:

In a separate bowl, combine the diced avocados, finely chopped red onion, diced cherry tomatoes, chopped cilantro, lime juice, salt, and pepper. Gently toss to combine, being careful not to mash the avocado too much. Adjust seasoning to taste.

3. Prepare the Tortilla Cups:

Preheat your oven to 375°F (190°C).
Lightly spray or brush both sides of the small tortillas with cooking spray or olive oil.
Gently press each tortilla into the cups of a muffin tin, forming small cups.
Bake in the preheated oven for 8-10 minutes, or until the tortillas are golden brown and crispy. Remove from the oven and let them cool slightly.

4. Assemble the Avocado Shrimp Cups:

Once the tortilla cups have cooled slightly, spoon a generous amount of the avocado mixture into each cup.
Top each cup with a cooked shrimp.
Garnish the avocado shrimp cups with cilantro leaves and serve with lime wedges on the side.

5. Serve:

- Arrange the avocado shrimp cups on a serving platter and serve immediately as a delicious and elegant appetizer.

These avocado shrimp cups are fresh, flavorful, and perfect for any occasion. They're sure to impress your guests with their vibrant colors and delicious taste. Enjoy!

**Chicken Caesar Salad Cups**

Ingredients:

For the Salad Cups:

- 12 wonton wrappers
- Cooking spray or olive oil

For the Caesar Salad:

- 2 cups cooked chicken breast, diced or shredded
- 1 cup romaine lettuce, finely chopped
- 1/4 cup grated Parmesan cheese
- 1/4 cup Caesar salad dressing (store-bought or homemade)
- 1/4 cup croutons, crushed
- Salt and pepper to taste

Optional Garnish:

- Additional grated Parmesan cheese
- Freshly ground black pepper
- Fresh parsley or chopped chives

Instructions:

1. Preheat the Oven:

- Preheat your oven to 350°F (175°C).

2. Prepare the Wonton Cups:

   Lightly grease a muffin tin with cooking spray or olive oil.
   Gently press one wonton wrapper into each muffin cup, shaping them into cups.
   Make sure the edges of the wrappers overlap the sides of the cups to create a
   cup shape.
   Lightly spray the tops of the wonton wrappers with cooking spray or brush with
   olive oil.

3. Bake the Wonton Cups:

- Place the muffin tin in the preheated oven and bake for 8-10 minutes, or until the wonton cups are golden brown and crispy. Keep an eye on them to prevent burning. Once done, remove from the oven and let them cool in the tin.

4. Prepare the Caesar Salad:

In a mixing bowl, combine the cooked chicken breast, finely chopped romaine lettuce, grated Parmesan cheese, and crushed croutons.
Add the Caesar salad dressing to the bowl and toss until everything is well coated. Season with salt and pepper to taste.

5. Assemble the Salad Cups:

Once the wonton cups have cooled slightly, spoon a portion of the Caesar salad mixture into each cup.
Optionally, garnish each salad cup with additional grated Parmesan cheese, freshly ground black pepper, and chopped parsley or chives for extra flavor and presentation.

6. Serve:

- Arrange the chicken Caesar salad cups on a serving platter and serve immediately as a delicious and convenient appetizer or snack.

These chicken Caesar salad cups are perfect for parties, gatherings, or even as a light meal. They're crispy, flavorful, and easy to customize with your favorite salad ingredients. Enjoy!

**Mini Crab Cakes with Lemon Aioli**

Ingredients:

For the Mini Crab Cakes:

- 1 pound lump crab meat, picked over for shells
- 1/2 cup breadcrumbs
- 1/4 cup mayonnaise
- 1 large egg
- 2 tablespoons chopped fresh parsley
- 2 tablespoons chopped green onions
- 1 tablespoon Dijon mustard
- 1 teaspoon Worcestershire sauce
- 1 teaspoon Old Bay seasoning
- Salt and pepper to taste
- Olive oil or cooking spray, for frying

For the Lemon Aioli:

- 1/2 cup mayonnaise
- 1 clove garlic, minced
- 1 tablespoon fresh lemon juice
- 1 teaspoon lemon zest
- Salt and pepper to taste

Optional Garnish:

- Fresh parsley or chives, chopped
- Lemon wedges for serving

Instructions:

1. Prepare the Crab Cakes:

   In a large mixing bowl, combine the lump crab meat, breadcrumbs, mayonnaise, egg, chopped parsley, chopped green onions, Dijon mustard, Worcestershire sauce, Old Bay seasoning, salt, and pepper. Gently mix until well combined.
   Form the crab mixture into small patties, about 2-3 inches in diameter.

2. Cook the Crab Cakes:

   Heat olive oil or coat a skillet with cooking spray over medium heat.

Carefully place the crab cakes in the skillet and cook for 3-4 minutes on each side, or until golden brown and heated through. You may need to cook them in batches to avoid overcrowding the skillet.

Once cooked, transfer the crab cakes to a plate lined with paper towels to drain any excess oil.

3. Make the Lemon Aioli:

In a small bowl, whisk together the mayonnaise, minced garlic, fresh lemon juice, lemon zest, salt, and pepper until smooth and well combined. Adjust seasoning to taste.

4. Serve:

- Arrange the mini crab cakes on a serving platter.
- Drizzle the lemon aioli over the crab cakes or serve it on the side for dipping.
- Garnish with chopped fresh parsley or chives and lemon wedges, if desired.

5. Enjoy:

- Serve the mini crab cakes with lemon aioli immediately as a delicious appetizer or party snack. They're sure to be a hit with your guests!

These mini crab cakes with lemon aioli are bursting with flavor and make for an impressive appetizer at any gathering. Enjoy the combination of tender crab meat with the tangy citrus kick of the aioli sauce!

**Greek Meatball Skewers with Tzatziki Sauce**

Ingredients:

For the Greek Meatballs:

- 1 pound ground lamb or beef
- 1/2 cup breadcrumbs
- 1/4 cup finely chopped red onion
- 2 cloves garlic, minced
- 1 tablespoon chopped fresh parsley
- 1 tablespoon chopped fresh mint (optional)
- 1 teaspoon dried oregano
- 1 teaspoon ground cumin
- 1/2 teaspoon ground coriander
- Salt and pepper to taste

For the Tzatziki Sauce:

- 1 cup Greek yogurt
- 1/2 cucumber, grated and squeezed to remove excess moisture
- 2 cloves garlic, minced
- 1 tablespoon chopped fresh dill
- 1 tablespoon lemon juice
- Salt and pepper to taste

For Skewering and Serving:

- Wooden or metal skewers, soaked in water if wooden
- Olive oil, for brushing
- Lemon wedges for serving
- Chopped fresh parsley or dill for garnish (optional)

Instructions:

1. Prepare the Greek Meatballs:

    In a large mixing bowl, combine the ground lamb or beef, breadcrumbs, finely chopped red onion, minced garlic, chopped fresh parsley, chopped fresh mint (if using), dried oregano, ground cumin, ground coriander, salt, and pepper.
    Mix the ingredients together until well combined.

Shape the mixture into small meatballs, about 1 inch in diameter.

2. Preheat the Grill or Oven:

- Preheat your grill to medium-high heat or preheat your oven to 400°F (200°C).

3. Skewer the Meatballs:

Thread the prepared meatballs onto the skewers, leaving a small space between each one.
Brush the meatballs with olive oil to prevent sticking and promote browning.

4. Grill or Bake the Skewers:

If grilling: Place the skewers on the preheated grill and cook for 10-12 minutes, turning occasionally, until the meatballs are cooked through and browned on all sides.
If baking: Place the skewers on a baking sheet lined with parchment paper and bake in the preheated oven for 15-20 minutes, or until the meatballs are cooked through and browned.

5. Make the Tzatziki Sauce:

In a medium bowl, combine the Greek yogurt, grated cucumber, minced garlic, chopped fresh dill, lemon juice, salt, and pepper. Stir until well combined.
Taste and adjust the seasoning as needed.

6. Serve:

- Remove the Greek meatball skewers from the grill or oven and let them rest for a few minutes.
- Serve the skewers hot with the tzatziki sauce on the side for dipping.
- Garnish with chopped fresh parsley or dill and serve with lemon wedges for squeezing over the meatballs.

7. Enjoy:

- These Greek meatball skewers with tzatziki sauce are best served hot and are perfect for a party appetizer or as part of a Greek-inspired meal. Enjoy the delicious flavors of the Mediterranean!

**Mini Sausage Rolls**

Ingredients:

For the Sausage Filling:

- 1 pound (450g) ground pork sausage
- 1 small onion, finely chopped
- 1 clove garlic, minced
- 1 teaspoon dried thyme
- 1 teaspoon dried sage
- Salt and pepper to taste

For the Pastry:

- 1 package (about 17.3 ounces or 490g) puff pastry, thawed if frozen
- All-purpose flour, for dusting
- 1 egg, beaten (for egg wash)

Instructions:

1. Preheat the Oven:

- Preheat your oven to 400°F (200°C). Line a baking sheet with parchment paper or silicone baking mat for easy cleanup.

2. Prepare the Sausage Filling:

In a large mixing bowl, combine the ground pork sausage, finely chopped onion, minced garlic, dried thyme, dried sage, salt, and pepper. Mix until well combined. Alternatively, you can use pre-seasoned ground sausage meat.

3. Roll out the Pastry:

On a lightly floured surface, roll out the puff pastry into a large rectangle, about 1/8 inch (3mm) thick.
Cut the pastry into smaller rectangles, about 2-3 inches wide and 4-5 inches long.

4. Assemble the Sausage Rolls:

Place a portion of the sausage filling along one edge of each pastry rectangle. Roll up the pastry tightly around the filling, sealing the edges by pressing them together.

Place the sausage rolls seam-side down on the prepared baking sheet.

5. Brush with Egg Wash:

- Brush the tops of the sausage rolls with beaten egg. This will give them a golden brown color when baked.

6. Bake:

- Place the baking sheet in the preheated oven and bake the sausage rolls for 20-25 minutes, or until they are golden brown and cooked through.

7. Serve:

- Once baked, remove the sausage rolls from the oven and let them cool slightly on the baking sheet.
- Transfer the sausage rolls to a serving platter and serve warm. They can be enjoyed on their own or with your favorite dipping sauce, such as ketchup or mustard.

8. Enjoy:

- These mini sausage rolls are best served fresh from the oven while still warm and crispy. They're perfect for any occasion and are sure to be a hit with family and friends!

Feel free to customize the sausage filling with your favorite herbs and spices, or add a touch of cheese for extra flavor. Enjoy your delicious homemade mini sausage rolls!

**Mushroom Bruschetta**

Ingredients:

- 1 French baguette, sliced into 1/2-inch thick rounds
- 1 pound (450g) mushrooms (such as cremini or button), cleaned and sliced
- 2 tablespoons olive oil
- 2 cloves garlic, minced
- 1 tablespoon fresh thyme leaves (or 1 teaspoon dried thyme)
- Salt and pepper to taste
- 1 tablespoon balsamic vinegar (optional)
- 1/4 cup chopped fresh parsley or basil, for garnish
- Grated Parmesan cheese, for serving (optional)

Instructions:

1. Prepare the Bread:

- Preheat your oven to 375°F (190°C). Place the baguette slices on a baking sheet in a single layer. Drizzle or brush the slices with olive oil. Bake in the preheated oven for about 10 minutes, or until the bread is golden and crispy. Remove from the oven and set aside.

2. Sauté the Mushrooms:

Heat 2 tablespoons of olive oil in a large skillet over medium heat.
Add the minced garlic to the skillet and cook for about 1 minute until fragrant.
Add the sliced mushrooms to the skillet and cook, stirring occasionally, until they are golden brown and tender, about 8-10 minutes.
Season the mushrooms with fresh thyme leaves, salt, and pepper. If desired, add a splash of balsamic vinegar for extra flavor. Stir to combine and cook for another 2-3 minutes.

3. Assemble the Mushroom Bruschetta:

Place a spoonful of the sautéed mushrooms on top of each toasted baguette slice.
Sprinkle chopped fresh parsley or basil over the mushrooms for garnish.
Optionally, sprinkle grated Parmesan cheese over the top for added flavor.

4. Serve:

- Arrange the mushroom bruschetta on a serving platter and serve immediately as a delicious appetizer or snack.

5. Enjoy:

- Enjoy the mushroom bruschetta while the bread is still warm and crispy. The savory mushrooms, fragrant garlic, and aromatic herbs create a delightful flavor combination that's perfect for any occasion.

Feel free to customize this recipe by adding other ingredients such as diced tomatoes, caramelized onions, or crumbled goat cheese. Experiment with different mushroom varieties to find your favorite combination. Enjoy your homemade mushroom bruschetta!

**Teriyaki Tofu Skewers**

Ingredients:

For the Teriyaki Sauce:

- 1/2 cup soy sauce
- 1/4 cup water
- 2 tablespoons brown sugar
- 2 tablespoons honey or maple syrup
- 2 cloves garlic, minced
- 1 teaspoon grated ginger
- 1 tablespoon cornstarch
- 2 tablespoons water

For the Tofu Skewers:

- 1 block firm or extra firm tofu, pressed and cut into cubes
- 2 bell peppers, cut into chunks
- 1 red onion, cut into chunks
- Wooden or metal skewers, soaked if using wooden

Optional Garnish:

- Toasted sesame seeds
- Sliced green onions
- Chopped cilantro

Instructions:

1. Prepare the Teriyaki Sauce:

   In a small saucepan, combine the soy sauce, water, brown sugar, honey or maple syrup, minced garlic, and grated ginger. Bring to a simmer over medium heat, stirring occasionally.
   In a small bowl, mix the cornstarch with 2 tablespoons of water to create a slurry. Stir the slurry into the saucepan with the simmering sauce.
   Cook for an additional 1-2 minutes, or until the sauce thickens slightly. Remove from heat and set aside.

2. Prepare the Tofu:

Press the block of tofu to remove excess water. You can do this by wrapping the tofu in a clean kitchen towel and placing a heavy object on top for about 30 minutes.
Cut the pressed tofu into cubes.

3. Assemble the Skewers:

Thread the tofu cubes, bell pepper chunks, and red onion chunks onto the skewers, alternating the ingredients.
Place the assembled skewers in a shallow dish or pan.

4. Marinate the Skewers:

Pour half of the teriyaki sauce over the skewers, making sure they are evenly coated.
Allow the skewers to marinate for at least 30 minutes, or longer for more flavor. You can refrigerate them if marinating for longer periods.

5. Grill or Bake the Skewers:

- Preheat your grill to medium-high heat or preheat your oven to 400°F (200°C).
- If grilling, place the skewers on the grill and cook for about 5-7 minutes on each side, or until the tofu is browned and the vegetables are tender.
- If baking, place the skewers on a lined baking sheet and bake in the preheated oven for about 20-25 minutes, flipping halfway through, until the tofu is browned and the vegetables are tender.

6. Serve:

- Remove the cooked skewers from the grill or oven and transfer them to a serving platter.
- Drizzle the remaining teriyaki sauce over the skewers.
- Garnish with toasted sesame seeds, sliced green onions, and chopped cilantro if desired.
- Serve hot as an appetizer or main dish with rice or noodles.

7. Enjoy:

- Enjoy these delicious teriyaki tofu skewers with your favorite sides and dipping sauce. They're perfect for a vegetarian barbecue or a flavorful weeknight meal!

**Cranberry Turkey Pinwheels**

Ingredients:

- 4 large flour tortillas
- 1/2 cup cream cheese, softened
- 1/4 cup mayonnaise
- 1/2 cup dried cranberries
- 1/2 cup chopped pecans
- 1/2 pound thinly sliced turkey breast
- 1 cup baby spinach leaves
- Salt and pepper to taste

Instructions:

Prepare the Filling:
- In a mixing bowl, combine softened cream cheese and mayonnaise until smooth.
- Stir in dried cranberries and chopped pecans. Season with salt and pepper to taste.

Assemble the Pinwheels:
- Lay out one tortilla on a flat surface.
- Spread a quarter of the cream cheese mixture evenly over the tortilla.
- Layer turkey slices over the cream cheese mixture, covering the entire surface.
- Place a handful of baby spinach leaves on top of the turkey.

Roll the Pinwheels:
- Starting from one edge, tightly roll up the tortilla.
- Repeat the process with the remaining tortillas and filling.

Chill and Slice:
- Once all tortillas are rolled, wrap them individually in plastic wrap.
- Refrigerate the wrapped rolls for at least 30 minutes to firm up.
- When ready to serve, remove the plastic wrap and slice each roll into 1-inch thick pinwheels.

Serve:
- Arrange the pinwheels on a serving platter.
- Garnish with additional cranberries and pecans if desired.
- Serve chilled and enjoy!

These cranberry turkey pinwheels are not only delicious but also visually appealing, making them a hit at any gathering. Feel free to customize the recipe by adding your favorite ingredients or adjusting the seasonings to suit your taste preferences.

**Mini Chicken Pot Pies**

Ingredients:

- 2 cups cooked chicken, diced or shredded
- 1 cup frozen mixed vegetables (carrots, peas, corn, green beans), thawed
- 1 cup chicken broth
- 1/2 cup milk
- 1/4 cup all-purpose flour
- 2 tablespoons unsalted butter
- 1/2 teaspoon garlic powder
- 1/2 teaspoon onion powder
- Salt and pepper to taste
- 1 package (2 sheets) store-bought puff pastry, thawed
- 1 egg, beaten (for egg wash)

Instructions:

Prepare the Filling:
- In a saucepan, melt butter over medium heat.
- Stir in flour and cook for 1-2 minutes until golden brown, stirring constantly.
- Gradually whisk in chicken broth and milk until smooth.
- Season with garlic powder, onion powder, salt, and pepper.
- Cook, stirring occasionally, until the mixture thickens, about 5 minutes.
- Stir in cooked chicken and mixed vegetables until well combined.
- Remove from heat and let the filling cool slightly.

Prepare the Pastry:
- Preheat your oven to 375°F (190°C).
- Roll out the thawed puff pastry sheets on a lightly floured surface.
- Using a round cookie cutter or a glass, cut out circles slightly larger than the openings of your mini muffin tin.
- Press each circle of pastry into the bottom and up the sides of greased mini muffin cups, forming mini pie crusts.

Fill the Pastry:
- Spoon the chicken and vegetable filling into each pastry-lined muffin cup, filling them almost to the top.

Top with Pastry:
- Cut out smaller circles of puff pastry to use as tops for the mini pies.
- Place each pastry circle on top of the filled muffin cups.
- Press the edges of the pastry together to seal, and crimp with a fork if desired.
- Brush the tops of the pies with beaten egg for a golden finish.

Bake:
- Place the mini muffin tin in the preheated oven and bake for 20-25 minutes, or until the pastry is golden brown and the filling is bubbly.

Serve:
- Allow the mini chicken pot pies to cool slightly before carefully removing them from the muffin tin.
- Serve warm and enjoy!

These mini chicken pot pies are not only adorable but also incredibly tasty, with flaky pastry and a savory, creamy filling. They're sure to be a hit at any gathering or as a comforting snack for the family.

**Smoked Gouda and Bacon Stuffed Mushrooms**

Ingredients:

- 24 large white mushrooms, cleaned and stems removed
- 6 slices of bacon, cooked and crumbled
- 1 cup smoked Gouda cheese, grated
- 1/4 cup breadcrumbs
- 2 cloves garlic, minced
- 2 tablespoons fresh parsley, chopped
- 2 tablespoons olive oil
- Salt and pepper to taste
- Cooking spray

Instructions:

Preheat the Oven:
- Preheat your oven to 375°F (190°C).

Prepare the Mushrooms:
- Remove the stems from the mushrooms and set them aside. Clean the mushroom caps with a damp paper towel to remove any dirt.

Prepare the Filling:
- Finely chop the mushroom stems.
- In a skillet, heat the olive oil over medium heat. Add the chopped mushroom stems and minced garlic. Cook until softened, about 3-4 minutes.
- Transfer the cooked mushroom stems and garlic to a mixing bowl.
- Add crumbled bacon, grated smoked Gouda cheese, breadcrumbs, chopped parsley, salt, and pepper to the bowl. Mix until well combined.

Stuff the Mushrooms:
- Place the mushroom caps on a baking sheet lined with parchment paper or aluminum foil, gill side up.
- Using a small spoon, fill each mushroom cap with the bacon and cheese mixture, pressing it down gently to pack it in.

Bake:
- Bake the stuffed mushrooms in the preheated oven for 15-20 minutes, or until the mushrooms are tender and the filling is golden brown and bubbly.

Serve:
- Once done, remove the stuffed mushrooms from the oven and let them cool slightly.
- Arrange the mushrooms on a serving platter and garnish with additional chopped parsley if desired.
- Serve warm and enjoy!

These smoked Gouda and bacon stuffed mushrooms are sure to impress your guests with their rich, savory flavor and creamy texture. They make a perfect appetizer for any occasion, from casual gatherings to elegant dinner parties.

**Chocolate-Dipped Strawberries**

Ingredients:

- Fresh strawberries, washed and dried
- Dark, milk, or white chocolate chips or bars (about 8 ounces)
- Optional toppings: chopped nuts, shredded coconut, sprinkles, or crushed candies

Instructions:

Prepare the Strawberries:
- Ensure that the strawberries are completely dry before dipping them in chocolate. Any moisture can cause the chocolate to seize.

Melt the Chocolate:
- Chop the chocolate bars into small, uniform pieces, if using.
- Place the chocolate chips or chopped chocolate in a microwave-safe bowl.
- Microwave the chocolate in 30-second intervals, stirring between each interval, until the chocolate is completely melted and smooth. Alternatively, you can melt the chocolate using a double boiler on the stove.

Dip the Strawberries:
- Hold a strawberry by the stem and dip it into the melted chocolate, swirling to coat it evenly.
- Lift the strawberry out of the chocolate and allow any excess chocolate to drip off.
- If desired, roll the chocolate-coated strawberry in optional toppings while the chocolate is still wet.

Set the Chocolate:
- Place the chocolate-dipped strawberries on a baking sheet lined with parchment paper or wax paper.
- Allow the chocolate to set at room temperature, or you can place the strawberries in the refrigerator for about 15-20 minutes to speed up the process.

Serve:
- Once the chocolate has set, arrange the chocolate-dipped strawberries on a serving plate or platter.
- Serve them immediately as a decadent dessert or romantic gesture.

Chocolate-dipped strawberries are best enjoyed fresh on the day they are made.

However, you can store any leftovers in the refrigerator for up to 24 hours, though the strawberries may start to release moisture over time. Enjoy these delightful treats as a luxurious indulgence or as a beautiful addition to any celebration.

Printed in the USA
CPSIA information can be obtained
at www.ICGtesting.com
CBHW081955241024
16238CB00037B/1256